THE
LESSON
PLAN

EDUCATIONAL • INSPIRATIONAL • METAPHORS
MOTIVATIONAL • SHORT STORIES

THE LESSON PLAN

A Workbook for Mothers & Teenage Daughters

GWEN Y. GISTARB

LitPrime
"Your story is our priority"

LitPrime Solutions
21250 Hawthorne Blvd
Suite 500, Torrance, CA 90503
www.litprime.com
Phone: 1-800-981-9893

Published by LitPrime Solutions   05/09/2023

ISBN: 979-8-88703-232-0(sc)
ISBN: 979-8-88703-233-7(e)

Loving My Mother

Oh, Mother, I love you, dear.
You are my first friend,
and I will keep you
nearby.

Peace within, I have learned from you.
Do not ever leave me.
I shall not know what to do.
Oh Mother, how shall I survive
without you close?
Your heart, your soul I need from you,
keeping me still until I know what to do.

Your loving daughter

FORWARD

MOTHER-DAUGHTER RELATIONSHIPS ARE SO precious and so important to our communities and to our society. Learning to listen to our daughters without being judgmental, motivating them, encouraging them to take care of themselves and not be dependent on romantic relationships, and incorporating technology as a parental teaching tool are just four examples of the valuable information mothers will find within this book.

The author, Gwen Gistarb, is a compassionate, amazing woman. She is a committed educator and is dedicated to improving the quality of life within our society. This book is filled with important, basic information that is easy to comprehend and relay on behalf of the mother-daughter relationship.

The Lesson Plan provides a wealth of information that should be shared in school settings, faith-based and community-based organizations, as well as correction agencies. The depth and quality of the information provided will absolutely enhance the lives and relationships of mothers and daughters, as well as those of readers.

This is a wonderful, enlightening work filled with hope and joy and written by a brilliant author, my dear friend Ms. Gwen Gistarb. To everyone—read, grow, learn, and enjoy.

—Marilyn K. Gambrell
Founder and CEO
No More Victims, Inc.

ACKNOWLEDGMENTS

THIS WORKBOOK WOULD NOT have been possible if my mother had not enforced the importance of love, family, and caring for others. Teaching by leading, she demonstrated by example what makes a strong woman and passed it on to her daughters. I appreciate her support in believing that education takes a person far in life and that it is a mother's responsibility to guide her daughters to success. Thank you, Mother, for all that you gave.

Thank you to my family, friends, and those who gave me input while I was writing this workbook.

A special thanks to Marilyn Gambrell for her support in my efforts to develop a workbook that will help mothers and daughters all over the world.

Thank you, Thea Drake with Expressionistic Designs, for working tirelessly to create a workbook that will attract and keep the attention of mothers and daughters as they work through re-establishing their relationships and guidance to prepare for success.

I appreciate the educational system for the experience it has allowed me to gain during my teaching career, as well as the opportunity it gave me to share with the youth of the world.

CONTENTS

INTRODUCTION

Objective:

the mother will... Understand that each of her daughters is as different as each new day.

PARENTING TECHNIQUES HAVE REMAINED the same for centuries. During the nineteenth century, most households included nuclear families. There were dads in the households to influence their sons as positive role models. Unlike in the nineteenth century, in the twenty-first century, single mothers raise their children alone. Women during the nineteenth century were successful in raising their boys to become men and their girls to become ladies. Unlike today, in the past, boys were trained as skilled workers to take care of their families, and girls were trained to take care of their households once they became adults. The process has changed since then. Today it is difficult for women to raise their sons without incident and to instill ladylike qualities in their daughters. It is quite confusing for parents to foster and teach family values when society and technology have become major competitors for children's attention in most households.

As the parent of a daughter and son, I have been given the opportunity to experience raising each. The rules my parents used were the ones I have also used. I understand some rules may or may not work depending on the personality of each child. As parents, we have learned the "how-to" from one generation to the next. Parenting is a difficult job because parents must take responsibility for preparing their children for society. The twenty-first-century, society is experiencing a lack of many character traits from teenagers because of poor parental leadership. This workbook will help guide *Mothers* through the responsibilities of proper parenting skills and the responsibilities teenagers must accept to become accountable.

The Lesson Plan is written to help achieve several parental objectives:

- re-building failing mother/daughter relationships
- listening without being judgmental
- incorporating technology as a parental teaching tool
- motivating your teenage daughter to positive thinking
- building self-esteem, self-awareness, self-confidence, and self-respect
- teaching reading, writing, and communication skills, as well as simple mathematics
- teaching teenagers how to prepare for the workforce
- sharing stories about teaching twenty-first-century teenage girls
- being a source of change
- building character
- making decisions
- becoming accountable
- accepting responsibility

Acquiring the title of *good parent* is a learning process. There are many resources available that will give you the basics for raising children, but much of the process is hands on, one step at a time, and one child at a time. Spacing children two to two and a half years apart will allow you to build a bond with each of them. Planning their futures and spending time learning their personalities will give you the opportunity to listen to and respect them just as they will listen and respect you. As children reach their teenage years, a great understanding of building a strong family should have been established by their parents. Teenagers accept guidance from parents who have built a strong family through:

- identifying ways to strengthen family relationships.
- identifying causes of family problems.
- discussing ways to solve family problems.
- identifying sources of outside help for family problems; and
- setting and enforcing house rules.

IMPORTANT QUALITIES OF BEING A PARENT

THE THREE MAIN FORCES behind parental responsibilities are exhibited in the following categories: dedication, nurturance, and flexibility. These powerful points are illustrated throughout this book through stories, poems, metaphors, lessons, and activities that will provide you the opportunity to bond with your daughters and begin to understand where they are at this point in their lives.

1. Dedication
   - Deep level of commitment – Must be prepared for a twenty-four-hour-a-day job.
   - Full-time position – This will require the parent to be always available for more than eighteen years.
   - Interrupted breakfast, lunch, dinner, and coffee breaks – Just when you think you have a moment for yourself, you may be needed, again.
   - Limited resignations – Because children require numerous expenses, job security is of the utmost importance.

2. Nurturance
   - Loving care and attention – Give each child your undivided attention.
   - Positive communication –Listening, then, answering, or responding when you are asked.
   - Encouragement - Being supportive even if you do not agree and using tact with corrective criticism.
   - Girl talk – Visit her bedroom (call it her apartment) striking up a conversation. Plan a mother-daughter day to hang out, doing some of what she wants to do.

3. Flexibility
   - Adaptability to a change in circumstances – Limit emotions to taking over when schedules are forced to change.

- Consideration of mood swings – Always remember that children have bad days too.
- Changes in daily routine – Be prepared for emergencies, illness, and the unexpected. Allowing flexibility in daily routines also allows room to share special moments.
- Unlimited budget - Unexpected expenses are always challenging. This position does not require you to be rich, but creating a budget is good practice.

Experience the fringe benefits of participating in a lifelong commitment of hearing my first words, watching me take my first steps, teaching me to ride my first bicycle, and watching with pride as I receive my high school and college diplomas.

To be considered for this lifetime opportunity, call for more information:

My First Everything, Inc.
1-800-For-Ever

Will You Be My Parent?

Look at me.
Don't you see my innocence?
I need guidance.
Will you be there for me?
I am confused and need you to share your wisdom.
Please be my leader
as I grow to share what you have taught me.
I just want a chance.
So, will you be my parent?

SEGMENT I

STAYING ON MY SIDE OF THE LINE

Objective:

The mother will... Identify the influences her daughters must contend with during their developmental stages.

There is a thin line between friendship and being a mother to your daughter.

Can you be both?

Parent | Friend

A Daughter's Best Friend

MOTHERS AND DAUGHTERS ARE warm and fuzzy. Mothers and daughters are beautiful. Mothers who can see themselves through their daughters hold a special feeling for a lifetime. Mothers and daughters grow to become best friends. Mothers are their daughters' first teachers-their daughters' first everything. Before a child's birth, the bond between mother and daughter has already been established. The relationship between mother and daughter is both friendly and respectful while being careful not to cross that thin line between the two so important words.

A daughter will always remember how far to go before crossing the line and a mother will always remind her daughter of the role she plays as a parent. Just like in a stage play, the two of you must stay connected to each prospective scene. In life, a mother's role is to teach from her life experiences, and a daughter should humbly welcome her mother's wisdom as she passes through the same challenges her mother did. Of course, raising a daughter is easier said, than done.

From the cradle, through the process, and to adolescence, a daughter begins to find her way, becoming friends with others and learning about her friends' households. These differing family norms may not be as structured as hers is. These differences could be a source of conflict between the mother and the daughter. Embracing the change of generations will require mothers to recognize the possibility of change within their relationships with their daughters.

After teaching your daughter morals, self-respect, building character, self-determination, and self-direction, a mother should then practice trust. Loosen the rope a little at a time to evaluate your daughter's obedience, let her demonstrate your teachings before you let go. Know that you are raising a good, respectful daughter, allowing her to find her way, and giving her room to come to you for motherly support.

Your daughter will challenge your authority when she begins to search for her own being. In the frustration of constantly competing for your place as the parent, you might begin to question your methods. You refer to when your mother raised you. You evaluate your personality and remember that the apple does not fall far from the tree. Although you may have tried, you never would have talked back to your mother in a disrespectful tone unless you wanted to never return from the floor ever again.

As you remember your youth, ask yourself, did you ever think that your daughter would do the same to you? Daughters today are quite different from daughters from earlier years when young women carried the title of "lady." Daughters are raised to act as ladies, and to always respect themselves without consideration of outside influence. They looked up to their mothers as role models. But today there are outside influences that are proven to be more challenging.

To stay connected, mothers and daughters must keep communication open in their relationship. It is interesting to know that each of us has two ears and one mouth. This might be so we can listen more and talk less. Mothers and daughters should find this important while understanding what is expected of each of them. Listening—really listening—is the most important part of effective communication. When mothers and daughters talk, mothers do most of the talking while daughters have their minds elsewhere, and they never get the full understanding of what their mothers are saying. For a change, mothers should allow their daughters to lead the conversation. Then, they both should come together in a summary of information for both.

Recognizing that your daughter is growing up will allow you to respect her decisions with more understanding responses. By telling her scenarios of similar situations you experienced in your youth, you will give her other options to compare and give her the chance to make a change in her life based on her decision. If you carefully step back to listen to her decision, you will reach a happy medium, and she will appreciate your input.

Mothers sometimes take the backseat when noticing their growing daughters are maturing into young ladies who want to do things for themselves. With your subtle input, your daughter will include you in her decisions. You will find that communicating in this manner will allow your daughter to feel responsible when she knows you are in her corner.

Mothers and daughters, most times will not agree on all subjects. Creating effective communication skills often prevents conflicts from developing. Practicing conflict resolution methods between mother and daughter will often get to the source of any problem and end with positive feelings between both.

As your daughter develops into the beautiful flower you created-first a young lady and then a young adult—the beauty is to see yourself in her. Carefully watch the wonderful relationship in which you steered your daughter to become your best friend and not just *your* best friend, but the person she will refer to as *her* best friend in return. What a wonderful feeling.

How to Improve Your Listening Skills

- keeping eye contact
- keeping an open mind
- listening to hear
- listening for meaning
- reflective listening
- listening without interruptions

Solutions to Resolve Conflict

- Take a deep breath.
- Ask yourself if you can ignore the situation.
- Identify why you are upset.
- Discuss how you feel without attacking each other.
- Listen with an open ear.
- Ask for what you want.
- Agree to disagree.
- Be open to compromise.

Retail Therapy

EXERCISE 1.1: QUESTIONS AND COMMENTS

The following questions are questions you should ask yourself, either as a mother or daughter:

1. List mother-daughter activities you can do together.
   a.
   b.
   c.

2. Identify which communication skills you need to improve.
   a.
   b.
   c.

3. How can you establish a positive relationship with your daughter/mother?
   a.
   b.
   c.

4. Mothers, how can you raise your daughter to be a lady?
   a.
   b.
   c.

5. When do you spend time together?
   a.
   b.
   c.

6. What do you do together?
   a.
   b.
   c.

7. Do you have girl talk? _____If so, what do you talk about?
   a.
   b.
   c.

8. Mothers, do you include yourself in conversations when your daughter(s) have friends over? _____ List ways you could include yourself.
   a.

b.

c.

9. Have you had the sex talk? _____ Mothers, how did you introduce the subject? What exactly did you say?

    a.

    b.

    c.

10. What about boys? Mothers, list three principal factors you will share with your daughter(s).

    a.

    b.

    c.

11. Daughter(s), list three important questions you have for your mother.

    a.

    b.

    c.

Write your own questions here:

_____

_____

_____

_____

_____

_____

_____

THE POWER OF INFLUENCE

UNDERSTANDING HOW CHILDREN GROW, develop, and mature allows parents to know what to realistically expect from their children. When parents listen to their children, they might say, "Who are they and where did they come from? Or will a mother say, "I am so proud of whom you have become," which means, you have done a great job. But when children are influenced by others, parents will need to intervene and exert control to communicate responsibilities.

Hopefully, your daughter will follow you, but some need more guidance than others. This is where your parenting skills take charge and are more demanding. Leading by example becomes a stronger force when raising more challenging children. In the first five years of a child's life, parents are their first teachers.

The knowledge of parenting will explain that each child is unique, and every child follows certain developmental patterns. The developmental stages include **Physical Development**, which refers to changes in a person's height, size, and weight.   The body's changes are the result of the growth of body muscle, bones, and tissue. **Intellectual Development** involves the progress in a person's mental and thinking abilities. This includes the development of a person's abilities in perception, attention, and association. Also, includes the ability to understand and use spoken and written language. Thinking, reasoning, and problem-solving skills are also included in this group. Learning to express emotions leads to **Emotional Development**, which recognizes feelings and emotions such as happiness, sadness, love, hate, anger, excitement, and fear. **Social Development** plays a significant role in personality development that is expressed through interactions with parents, siblings, friends, and others.

With much influence in this generation, parents' leadership is the most effective key to success. While keeping in mind that the strong forces before each of you will constantly require guidance.

INFLUENCES

So, what are your teenagers' influences, and what causes them? Consider the following examples:

Sibling Rivalry
- Too Close in Age
- Middle Child
- Different Daddies
- Personality Conflicts

Peer Pressure
- Personality Conflicts
- Boyfriend/Girlfriend Pressures
- Jealousy
- Puberty
- Group Leadership
- Sexual Pressures

Television
- Violence
- Drugs and Guns
- Sexually Explicit Primetime Shows
- Big Screen Movies

Music Industry
- Faddish Clothing
- Seductive/Sexual Music Videos
- Violence
- Vulgar Dance
- Profanity

EXERCISE 1.2: IDENTIFY YOUR TEENAGER'S INFLUENCES

Now, together with your daughter, use this page to identify her influences. Then, list the changes you will make to change her focus, if any.

Mother--what are your daughter's influences?

_____

_____

_____

_____

_____

_____

_____

_____

Daughter--what will you do to correct your influences?

_____

_____

_____

_____

_____

_____

_____

_____

What changes will you both make?

1. _____
2. _____
3. _____
4. _____
5. _____
6. _____
7. _____
8. _____
9. _____
10. _____

How will you compromise on these changes? Take notes here.

_____

_____

_____

_____

_____

_____

_____

_____

_____

_____

_____

_____

EXERCISE 1.3: TERMS TO KNOW

Mother, together with your daughter, define the terms below. Talk about how each of the words affects both of you.

Commitment	
Cultural traditions	
Heritage	
Influences	
Jealousy	
Moral development	
Morals	
Personal priorities	
Personalities	
Puberty	
Responsibilities	
Self-esteem	
Self-respect	

SEGMENT II

MY PLATE RUNNETH OVER

Objective:

The mother will... Identify the source of change in the twenty-first century teenagers.

In many cases,

Your **CONDITIONS**

plus Your **HABITS**

May determine your

"ATTITUDE"

The decision is yours...

To Much To Think About

EARNING A HIGH SCHOOL diploma, or its equivalent, has become more difficult to achieve all over the world. High school success lays the foundation for all teens whose plans are to succeed in society. As a parent and high school teacher, when I interviewed other educators, the poll was unanimous when I asked, "What did you think contributes to the problem of change within the teenage generation?" As you may notice throughout this book, teenagers still need their parent's guidance.

Non-Organizational Skills

Teens creating structured organizational skills will help them meet school deadlines and still have time for work and other social activities. It is recommended that students have a compact agenda planner so as requirements are presented, they can write in their planners. Electronic devices are not allowed in class so having a planner is the most efficient method for daily responsibilities. Posting a large wall calendar is another method for keeping up with assignments, projects, and other important appointments.

Home Assignments

Other than working on home assignments, your daughters would prefer doing fun activities. Setting homework rules and requiring your girls to complete home assignments first before playing would allow them more time for evening television programs and other extra-curricular activities before bedtime. It would be an innovative idea for schools to incorporate a study hall period just for home assignments so that those that work after school would have plenty of time for study.

School & Social Activities

As seen, girls are generally less able to separate themselves from teen social confusion and focus on schoolwork rather than boys, although many boys are just as caught up in the drama as girls. Regardless of what you may think, Mothers still have a great deal of influence over what their daughters believe about their talents and goals.

Listen to your daughters about what they are enthusiastic about, what they are good at, and how these might translate into careers. Guide them to understand that doing well academically can make these dreams a reality in their future.

Explaining the Link between Education and Financial Security

In earlier years girls who barely got by with their academic coursework during high school were able to find decent jobs when they graduated, but that is not the case today. If teenagers want to find careers in a satisfying, well-paying profession, they must apply themselves academically. In an increasingly competitive and technology-heavy workforce, most high school graduates will need at least two additional years of schooling (college or technical training) to land a decent job.

Guide your daughter to the Occupational Handbook, (found in the public library or online) which can explain the various job clusters. These entries will help your daughter to better understand the pay scale for each given profession. Research the Census Bureau for a breakdown of each level of degree and their financial future.

Senior Crunch Time

In past years, by senior year, girls had their required academic requirements out of the way. College acceptance letters had begun to arrive, and they could safely "slack off" a little. Not anymore! Today, many seniors are still working on some of their academic courses needed for graduation, state testing requirements are not being met and graduation is last minute on the line. Receiving a preliminary college acceptance letter doesn't mean they're off the hook academically since more and more colleges are withholding final acceptance based on end-of-senior year grades.

Too Many Irons in the Fire

Too much to do with not enough time will and can cause teenage girls to fail at the most important aspect of their lives. Having and maintaining a punctual scheduled planner is a sure method for them to participate in activities in and outside of school. In fact, extracurricular activities have many benefits.

However, this assumes that teenagers aren't spreading themselves so thin that they aren't making the best of their time.

Work Responsibility Too Soon

It appears to teens that by having a part-time job can spell freedom in the form of money for a car, clothing, cell phone, or other personal items. But, when girls begin work responsibilities too young or too much, school requirements are likely to be pushed to the back burner. As they try to earn still more money to pay for car insurance, repairs and gas, girls don't always realize that employers expect them to show up for work whether they've studied or not. Steering your enterprising teenager toward youth-friendly employers-more and more requires proof that girls are maintaining their grades-this might be the best way to help your enterprising daughters to maintain their education as their priority.

EXERCISE 2.1 WORDS OF THE HEART ACTIVITY

From the following list, identify twenty-five words that describe the relationship between you and your daughter. Then write sentences using those words.

Happiness	Sadness	Anger	Eagerness	Doubtfulness
calm	unhappy	irritated	earnest	unbelieving
satisfied	depressed	enraged	aggressive	skeptical
comfortable	dismal	furious	willingness	distrustful
joyous	blah	annoyed	zealous	suspicious
ecstatic	discouraged	inflamed	intent	uncertain
enthusiastic	disappointed	provoked	anxious	hesitant
inspired	embarrassed	indignant	keen	indecisive
grateful	ashamed	irate	hyper	powerless
peaceful	useless	bitter	nervous	defeated
spirited	worthless	frustrated	impatience	confused
Fearless	**Interested**	**Affectionate**	**Hurt**	**Physical**
encouraged	fascinated	tender	injured	taut
daring	intrigued	soft	isolated	paralyzed
confident	inquiring	desirous	offended	tired
brave	excited	warm	distressed	empty
heroic	curious	loving	suffering	strong
determined	absorbed	seductive	aching	weak
secure	engrossed	close	crushed	breathless
independent	concerned	passionate	heartbroken	nauseated
reassured	sincere	open	upset	sluggish
courageous	inquisitive	sexy	tortured	hard

WRITE YOUR SENTENCES HERE:

1. _____
2. _____
3. _____
4. _____
5. _____
6. _____
7. _____
8. _____
9. _____
10. _____
11. _____
12. _____
13. _____
14. _____
15. _____
16. _____
17. _____
18. _____
19. _____
20. _____
21. _____
22. _____
23. _____
24. _____
25. _____

Change is good,

but, it depends on the

DIRECTION

you are headed.

EXERCISE 2.2: WRITING ASSIGNMENT

Both you and your daughter can write an essay or a poem. Title your daughter's project, "Life as a Teenager and yours should be entitled, My Responsibilities as a Parent." This project can be long or short if it is complete. Then, you should talk about it, while this may help you to understand each of your roles. Include some of the feeling words from the previous page. Add to the list if necessary. Make this activity fun and maybe a race to see who will finish first.

Mother

_____

_____

_____

_____

_____

_____

_____

_____

_____

_____

_____

_____

_____

_____

_____

_____

_____

_____

_____

_____

_____

_____

_____

_____

_____

_____

_____

_____

_____

_____

_____

A mother is the closest link to her daughter's future, and it is the mother's responsibility to be her daughter's safety net if she should fall.

—A. S. Davis

Communication Skills

Speaking

Listening

Hearing

Segment III

I'm Here, When You Need Me

Objective:

the mother will... Determine the needs of her daughter while listening to the demands of what is required.

Listening is the most important aspect for building an open relationship between a mother and daughter.

—Brenda, Parent

Can I Talk To You?

From the moment of conception, you promised to love and guide me.
You said you'd navigate the way,
so why am I doing all the steering?

Now, I am a teenager in the prime of my life, and I need answers.
I need to talk to you, but you are not there.
What will I do?
I feel alone.

Mom, do you hear me?
I'm calling your name.
You decided to give me life,
so, please give me my future.

Whether in the same house or separate from my father,
I will need your guidance.
I'm still calling your name. Answer me.

Don't you hear me?
Mom, I need a role model.
Whom shall it be?

I thought the job was yours, so where are you?
It's storming out here, and I'm calling your name.
Let me in. I need you to hold my hand.

But oh, you let go, and oh too soon.
I still need you. Please answer me.
I'm not ready yet.

I still need to talk to you.

—Gwen Gistarb

CONFUSED

TEENAGERS ARE TIRED OF adults telling them about the good old days. Sure, it might seem like the right thing to say, but they're tired of hearing it. When I tell my students stories about the way things were years ago, their response is, "Adults should respect what is happening in our generation." This is true, but many of the things taking place in their generation are just not acceptable. How do you give respect to those who don't seem to respect themselves? Surely parents cannot be teaching their children to display the types of behavior I see daily. Or is it that children are just not being corrected at home and their disrespectful behavior is all they know?

Because children are faced with so many more issues today than we were as children, I sometimes feel out of place. Maybe adults just don't understand what young people are faced with, given they have so much more baggage than we did growing up. They don't only have school to contend with, but also raising themselves, raising their siblings, and even working to help pay the household bills. They are experiencing a lot of issues that I can't imagine where I would start if I had their responsibilities.

Today's children are having a difficult time understanding exactly what their roles are. One minute they are treated like children, and the next they are placed in an unfamiliar place of adulthood, not truly understanding exactly what they are supposed to do.

Are we placing too much pressure on our children? Yes, we are. How can we prepare them for their futures if we are demanding more than they are capable of understanding? Our children need more time to grow up. Why are we pushing so hard?

Understanding but still not understanding, my heart becomes heavy when my students talk about their homes. I must say that I do respect many of them because they just don't seem to have the family structure I did. After listening to their concerns, it is understandable why they do so poorly in school. With so much on their minds, it's amazing they even show up.

With so many daily decisions to make, it is understandable why children are choosing the wrong paths in their lives. Without guidance, how will they know? It takes a village to raise a child, the old saying goes, but when the village is scarce, it leaves room for the children to make major mistakes.

A SECOND CALL TO DUTY

GRANDMA, WHO ARE MY parents? I grew up with my grandmother because my parents left me with her as an infant. I don't know my parents. I still remember the first time I saw my mom when I was six years old. I remember when she came to visit, and when she walked up to me, I started to cry. Then, I asked my grandma, "Why did that lady want to hug me?" She said, "That lady is your mother." I was little and didn't understand because the only mom I had known was my grandmother. And now that I've gotten older, I want to know who I am, but no one will tell me.

—Susan A.

Children are the most precious gift that God
will give to a parent in a lifetime.

—Gwen Gistarb

A SECOND CHANCE

FIVE YEARS AGO, I wished I could have changed my dad. It was my mother's birthday, January 24. We were having so much fun with all of my family who had come over to celebrate such a special day when the telephone rang and my mother answered. It was a woman asking for my dad. When he noticed my mother's facial expression, he got nervous and asked what was wrong. At that moment, my mother discovered my dad was having an affair. It was an awful experience. I can remember me and my mother crying most of the night.

After a few weeks passed, my mother forgave my dad, and I got very angry with disappointment. I didn't understand why she would take him back. Now, that I've gotten older, I understand better that people make a lot of mistakes and that everyone deserves a second chance.

—Jamie

If you teach them, they will learn a lifetime of knowledge.

—Jacqui L.

WHEN CHILDREN LISTEN

W HEN MY SON AND daughter were teenagers, I can remember one of their conversations about going to college. My son seemed to have had his mind made up that he was not going to college, and before I could jump in, my daughter said, "You must not know who your parents are." So, without question, he finished college.

—Gwen Gistarb

A Parent's Responsibility

My Scratch-Off Miracle

O NE DAY I FOUND myself in difficult situation-between paychecks, not a dime to my name (literally), clients scheduled for the day, and a child to feed that night. As I searched the refrigerator for something to create for dinner that night and contemplated how far I could get on the fumes in my car, I decided to have a little talk with God.

I asked that no matter how big or small, I needed a financial miracle that day. I knew if I had even stumbled upon five dollars, it would have made a significant difference that day. Then on faith, I confirmed my clients and proceeded to go to my office with hope and a prayer that I would make it. On my drive, I decided that instead of focusing on the things that I didn't have, I would give thanks for the things I did. I needed to get myself in a better place mentally before meeting with anyone anyway.

Then, as I pulled into the parking area of my office, I got a phone call from a radio station. The woman on the line verified my information and asked if I had entered a drawing over the holidays. I totally had forgotten about it until she mentioned it. The drawing happened to be for a holiday basket from Central Market that I had planned to give to someone as a Christmas gift. No need for that now, I thought to myself, but as she proceeded with the conversation, I learned that I had won $45 in scratch-off lottery tickets. Now, if you're thinking, oh wow, she must have won millions, think again. But I did win $15, which paid for gas that day and a hot meal for my daughter that night. Remember to always keep the faith and that no matter how big or small, God can always work miracles.

—Shana

"Is it better to try and fail, or not try at all?"

A FACE IN THE MIRROR

THERE WERE MANY DAYS when I looked in the mirror and failed to even know my own face. A reflection with a lost troubled soul behind it, eyes filled more with a well understood since of struggle as if my life could be summed into one shallow small puddle. The child is lost within the depths of her own mind searching for compassion rather than lies. They say life is what you make of it and to be something great you shouldn't wait for placement. Only I could have uplifted myself from the shadows down at the bottom of a dark well, I called hard times. I believe being able to fully be re-born is way more than just a frame of mind. I now understand my own perception of the many different angles that shape real life. I try with a smile to be the very best I can as well as be able to grasp the true definition of being fully able to call myself a real girl. Understanding an individual with purpose because I know when it's all said and done, I would have accomplished just exactly everything I was placed on this earth for and nothing else.

—Gwen Gistarb

PARENTING IS A COMMITMENT

T IS IMPORTANT TO understand the qualifications required for the job of parenting. Listed below are words that will identify the job description profile for each area that a parent will fulfill. After reading each of the qualifications, complete the story on the next page.

A Parent is:

Teacher	A child's first connection to learning.
Health Provider	Monitor rest and exercise schedule. Keep appointments for proper vaccinations and is aware of symptoms of illnesses.
Caregiver	Constant care 24/7.
Nutrition Provider	Provides the proper diet at scheduled feeding times.
Cleanliness Director	Guidance for personal hygiene and clean environment.
Clothing Provider	Responsible for providing clothing for protection and comfort.
Safety-Guard	Provides an environment for children to grow and develop.
Guidance Provider	Provides guidelines and structure while allowing freedom within the structure.
Communicator	Communicates love through touch and words.
Educational Provider	Provides your children with an educational environment that supports their needs.
Supporter	Demonstrates morals, self-respect, self –esteem and to feel good about themselves. Provides love and support.

Social Director	To gain knowledge of social skills. Good manners and sharing.
Resource Person	Provide information and answer questions without boredom.
Chauffeur	Transport children for appointments and other activities.
Empathizer	Be considerate of your children's feelings.
Assistant Decision Maker	Support children in making decisions. Teach the decision-making process for all decisions to be made.

EXERCISE 3.1: PARENTING ACTIVITY

Directions: Using the words from the previous page, complete the activity below.

Upon making the decision to become a parent, there are many responsibilities one will encounter. In the beginning you will be responsible for providing constant care for your child 24 hours a day, seven days per week, and three hundred sixty-five days a year. You will now be referred to as a _____. As your child begins to develop her own personality and learns from all aspects of life, you are responsible for providing structure and guidance while allowing freedom within that structure. This makes you the _____ _____ in the home. When taking on such an important task, mothers creatively demonstrate many roles in their daughters first years. Parents are the first _____ their child will know, providing an enthusiastic attitude toward learning activities. Preparing your child with the best possible educational environment that matches their needs will support your efforts as an _____ _____. As a _____ _____, you will also provide social activities for your child, which will help them to gain knowledge of social skills such as sharing and good manners. Also, acting as a communicator, your child will know that they are loved through both words and touch. Speaking to them in a pleasant voice, rather than a bossy demanding tone will allow you to listen to their every concern. Being an _____, that is to be understanding and being considerate of children's feelings. Understanding outburst of anger and crying can help them deal with everyday issues better regardless of its magnitude. Many parents aren't aware that they are their child's main _____ _____. You must answer the many questions they may have, being patient and understanding. You are also responsible for maintaining proper schedules of rest and exercise for your child as well as vaccinations and always aware of the symptoms of illness, can perform first aide and be prepared to obtain medical services if needed. Basically, you are their _____ _____. Providing nutritious foods at properly scheduled feeding times and aware of their nutritional needs as they develop will require your expertise as a _____. You are the _____ in their lives. You are to help your child in making decisions, teaching them the decision-making process. Only to assist, allowing them to arrive at their own decision. You are their _____, providing them with clothing that is comfortable, allows movement, and provides protection from the elements. You also teach them cleanliness and how to maintain a clean environment. For many years your title among others, you will also be their _____, transporting your child to the doctor, school, parties, and many other activities as they grow. Demonstrate positive self-esteem by helping your child to feel good about who she is. Always providing support and love, whether she achieves or fails. Support her desire to try again. This will surely demonstrate that you are her _____. Parents should _____-_____ their children to provide a safe environment for growth and development.

SEGMENT IV

THE 100 PERCENT RULE

Objective:

the mother will...
Teach her daughter that the
decisions made in her life could become a
lifelong commitment.

JUST

say YES....

"ABSTINENCE"

Identify your problem

Examine your choices

Make your choice

Act on your decision

Evaluate your decision

FORCED TO GROW UP
A TEENAGE FATHER

IT WAS 12:30 IN the morning when my phone started to ring. I was cozy in my bed, so I ignored it. It kept on ringing and ringing, repeatedly until it stopped, then, the house phone started to ring, and my mom answered. She came into my room to wake me. Hurriedly, she woke me and said, "your girlfriend's water has broken, and they are on the way to the hospital."

My heart was beating like a set of drums at a football game. I said, "Let's go!" We got into the car, my dad driving and my mother in the passenger seat and as I sat in the back nervously as hell, I looked at them to see the excitement on their faces. I'd waited nine months and that little person is about to arrive.

When I got to the hospital, I could not find the delivery room and, of course, I got really frustrated. I asked a doctor in passing, but he wouldn't tell me until I told him I was about to be a Daddy. Being so excited I didn't hear him when he told me which elevator to take, I just found the stairs and ran up five floors.

I did finally make it to the delivery room where I was able to see the birth of my baby. This was the happiest moment in my life, and I can remember it as though it was yesterday. A beautiful baby girl!

I'm not quite ready, but I'm forced to grow up.

—Todd D.

HUMAN REPRODUCTION

UNDERSTANDING HUMAN REPRODUCTION BEGINS with family planning decisions. Knowing how babies are made will help you understand the importance of planning when couples want to expand their families. Explained below is a brief version of the reproduction process of the male and female.

> Reproduction develops sexually. With two sex cells as the source of reproduction, the **sperm** is delivered from the male and the **egg** is provided by the female. The sperm and egg unite to form a fertilized egg. The fertilized egg, then divides millions of times to form a human being. Men and women have required roles in reproduction.

The Man's Role

Figure 4.1 The Male Reproductive System:

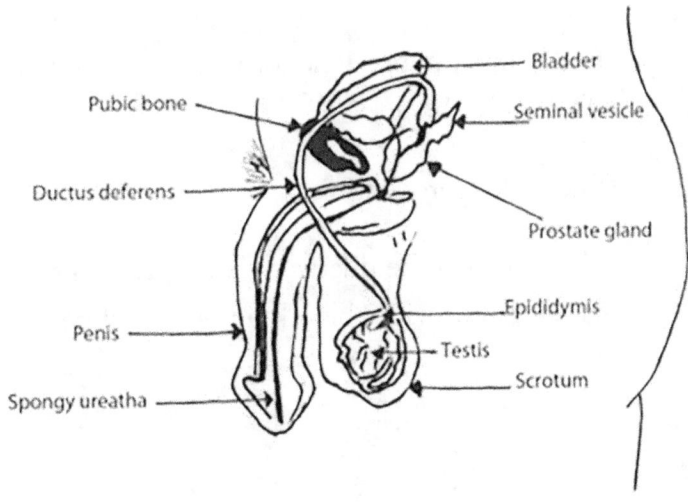

A male's role in reproduction is to produce **sperm** he will deliver to the female. Production of sperm begins in a man at puberty and continues throughout his lifetime. By the time a young man reaches adulthood, he will produce millions of sperm each month. It is produced and stored in the man's two **testes or testicles**.

Below are terms that will explain the man's sex organs:

Epididymis	Coil that is next to the testes where sperm is matured after passing through a series of ducts.
Vas Deferens	Long narrow tube attached to the *epididymis*. Sperm are carried through to the *vas deferens* up into the man's body-leading to an *ejaculatory duct*.
Urethra	The *urethra* extends through the penis where sperm leave the body.
Semen	Secretions from three sets of glands are added to the sperm as they reach the urethra. The secretions and sperm together are called *semen*. It is semen that leaves the male's body through ejaculation during sexual intercourse.
Scrotum	The sac contains the testes, blood vessels, and part of the spermatic cord.
Penis	The organ of copulation and urination in the male.
Prostate Gland	A firm partly muscular chestnut-sized gland in males at the neck of the urethra.
Testes	One of the two oval gonads (reproductive gland), is located in the cavity of the scrotum.
Seminal Vesicle	A structure in the male that is about two inches long and is located behind the bladder and above the prostate gland.
Pubic Bone	The body of pubic bone forms the wide strong medial and flat portion of the pubic bone.
Sperm	The male reproduction cell.
Ductus Deferens	The artery to the ductus deferens, as its name suggests, is an artery in males that provides blood to the vas deferens.

The Woman's Role

Figure 4.2 The Female Reproductive System:

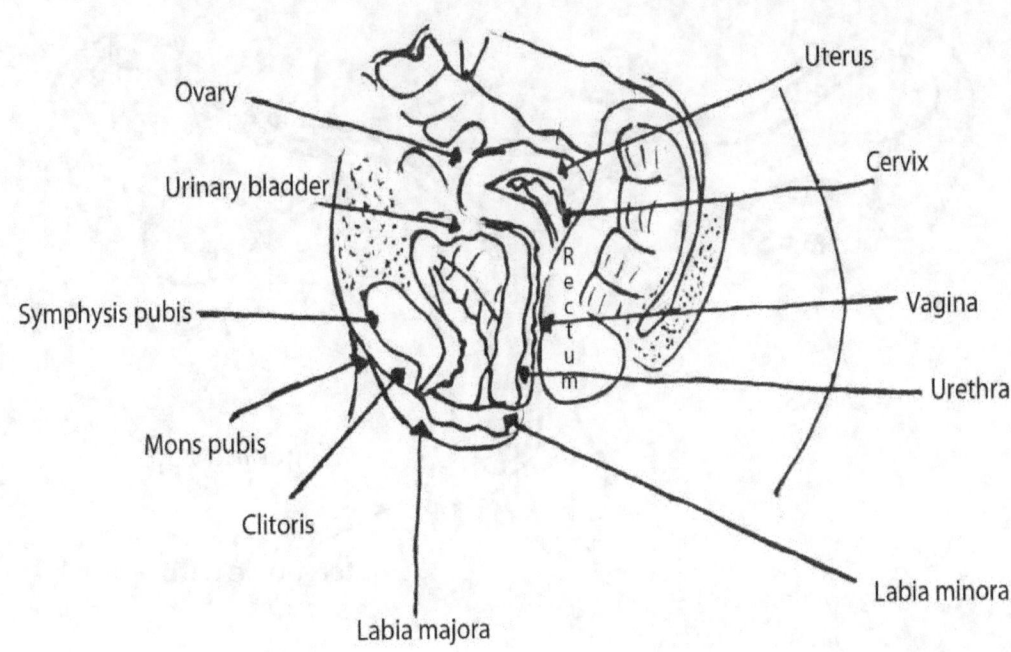

The role of the female in reproduction is to provide eggs and to carry and nourish a fertilized egg within her body until a baby is born. A female is born with about 400,000 immature egg cells. Unlike the male, her body does not produce any more eggs after she is born.

The eggs are stored in her two **ovaries** where only one egg is usually released from the ovaries each month. This process will start at **puberty**, then end at **menopause**. One egg is released from the ovaries through **ovulation**, which occurs about once a month. When leaving the ovary, the egg is passed into one of two tubes called the **fallopian tubes**. One end of each tube lies close to an ovary and the other end of the tube attaches to the **uterus**, which is a hollow muscular organ. These eggs will spend approximately three to four days traveling through the fallopian tube to the uterus. This egg is only fertile for only about a day after ovulation when sperm must meet the egg as it is in the fallopian tube to achieve fertilization. It is possible that sperm can survive in a woman's body for as long as three days. Upon the egg leaving the fallopian tube, it will then enter the uterus where it will hold and nourish a fertilized egg as it develops into a baby during pregnancy.

Each month the inner lining of the uterus thickens and develops a large network of tiny blood vessels called the endometrium. An unfertilized egg in the **endometrium** passes out through the uterus, leaving the body through the vagina in a process called **menstruation**.

The Process of Conception

Figure 4.3

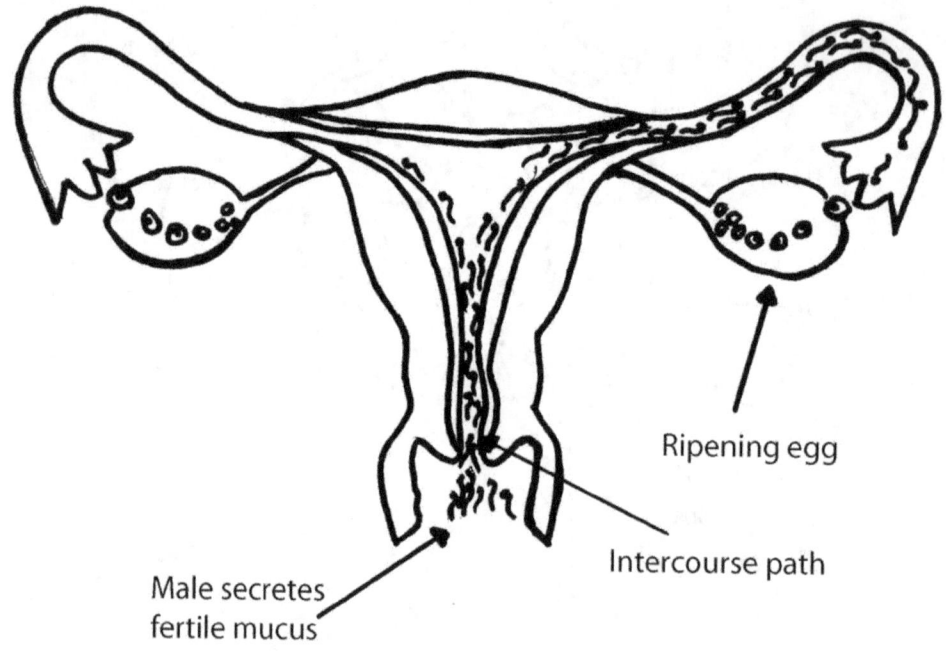

Ripening egg

Intercourse path

Male secretes
fertile mucus

The female body is designed to accept fertilization. Understanding the process will help when you are prepared for motherhood. For conception to occur an egg will be present, which is released when a woman ovulates. This process is called ovulation. A mature egg breaks away from the ovary, then travel down the fallopian tube and is ready for fertilization.

Between eleven to twenty-one days after the first day of a woman's menstrual period ovulation is stimulated by the pituitary gland's release. The conception will most likely occur around the time of ovulation. Sperm can live inside the female body for up to 72 hours (three days), but each mature egg can only be fertilized for 12 to 24 hours after it is released from the ovary.

SAFETY IN ABSTINENCE

I T IS IMPORTANT THAT you are fully aware of the dangers when you decide to become sexually active. There is safety in practicing abstinence until you are married and ready to be responsible for your sexual being. What is abstinence? This means not having sexual intercourse. Abstaining from sex until marriage will also give teenage girls time to grow socially and emotionally mature. Teaching daughters that mature people are better able to handle the responsibilities of sexual relationships with their partners.

Ideally, mothers and their teen daughters should be able to talk openly about sex. That is if you have developed an open relationship with her; one in which she can discuss anything with you. If not, this subject will be difficult to talk about. Your daughters need guidance and support from you to understand sexual issues. They also need information about their physical and sexual maturity. Mothers can too direct their daughters to factual sources of information via the internet, schools, community organizations, and religious groups that provide educational sessions about sexuality. Mothers and daughters may be able to attend such sessions together.

Practicing abstinence is the best method to use for teenage girls to not allow themselves to become a statistic, about teen pregnancy or STD lists. Below is a list of many known sexual diseases or STDs with which you should familiarize yourself. Some of these are more harmful than others and should be discussed with your daughter.

What are sexually transmitted diseases (STDs)?

Sexually transmitted diseases (STDs) are infections that can be transferred from one person to another through any type of sexual contact. STDs are sometimes referred to as sexually transmitted infections (STIs) since they involve the transmission of a disease-causing organism from one person to another during sexual activity. It is important to realize that sexual contact includes more than just sexual intercourse. Sexual contact includes kissing, oral-genital contact, and the use of sexual "toys," such as vibrators. The most dangerous of these conditions is acquired immunodeficiency syndrome (AIDS)." (Medicine.net)

List of Most Common Sexually Transmitted Diseases

- Chancroid
- Chlamydia
- Genital Herpes
- Gonorrhea
- Human Immunodeficiency Virus (HIV) and Acquired Immuno-deficiency Syndrome (AIDS)
- Human Papillomaviruses (HPVs) and Genital Warts
- Syphilis

Responsibility

Respect

Commitment

I SHOULD HAVE WAITED

I WAS 16 AND A sophomore in high school when I had so many things planned for my junior year. This is when I made one bad decision and everything, I had planned went down the drain. I got pregnant in October 2008. I was so afraid and didn't know what to do. I didn't tell anyone except the father. Because I was in denial about being pregnant, I didn't take a pregnancy test until December. I was scared to look at the test and when I did the two lines indicated what I already knew, I was pregnant. I text my boyfriend and told him I was 99% sure I was pregnant. When I got home my sister asked me if I was pregnant because I was going to the restroom a lot and she knew the signs. She told my mom that she thought I was pregnant. Not giving me the chance to tell my mother in my own time, she forced me to tell her. When I told her, she was very angry with me. I was kind of surprised that she took it this way because I had told her when I lost my virginity. This would have been the time she should have spoken to me about the consequences of having sex, but she didn't. I guess she didn't think it was important at the time. I wish she would have taken the time to speak with me about it. The only thing she told me was not to do it again, as if that was enough. I don't blame my mother for my decision, but I felt that as a mother she should have said more.

During this time, we were living with my mom's boyfriend, and we didn't get along, but I would try to be nice to him just to make my mom happy. Shortly after I found out I was pregnant I left to live with my stepdad because of the problems between me and my mother. I didn't speak to her for a very long time. So, the only one I had to help me through this very hard time was my baby's father and his family. His mom would bring me food because my stepdad was never home, and I was left with hardly any food in the house. He wasn't much help to me at all.

My boyfriend and his mother took me to Planned Parenthood. By this time, I was about 4 months pregnant and wasn't sure what I was going to do. If I wasn't going to be living with my mom, how would I take care of this baby all alone? How will I get food for me and the baby? So many things were going through my head that I didn't know what to think. The people at Planned Parenthood told me that I was close to 15 weeks pregnant and if abortion was the solution, my time was running out. Yeah, I thought about having an abortion, not because I didn't want to keep my baby, but because I knew I wouldn't be able to care for it. When I left there, I arranged a doctor's appointment and was given an ultrasound when I learned that I was having a girl. At this point, I couldn't get rid of her. I talked with my boyfriend's family, and we concluded that I would keep my little girl and move in with them in the summer.

Around the time I was 6 months I moved back in with my mom and suddenly things were getting better. I thought being with my mother was the best thing for me during this time, but I still wanted to move with my boyfriend. After moving back in with my mom up to my 8th month I would have arguments with my sister. Even though I was pregnant she would argue with my mom about me so that I wouldn't go to my boyfriend's house. I would cry a lot during that time. The day of my baby shower my mom made a big scene because she asked me where the presents were going to go and, "I said to my boyfriend's house." She got so angry and started saying ugly things to me. She was already aware this was where they were going, but obviously just wanted to start an argument with me. She stormed out and left. We didn't talk for a week, but things soon returned to normal.

A month later I moved to my boyfriend's house because we were getting kicked out of our apartment mom was moving back in with her boyfriend and my sister was going with her. It's been six weeks since I had been living with his family. On the day of my due date, which was June 29, 2009, I started having contractions beginning about five in the morning. They were far apart in the early morning. I had a checkup at 9 AM and when I went in my doctor told me I was dilated to 3cm and that she would see me that night. This is when I begin to get excited. I could only think about by nightfall I was going to be holding my baby girl in my arms. For the entire day, which was a Monday, once returning home I walked around with the contractions. I took a shower around 5 pm and at around 6 pm I went to the restroom, and I noticed that there was a small stain. I told my boyfriend and his mom, and she told me she didn't think it was my water because it was supposed to be a lot. So, I just waited, at around 8 pm family started coming over and I was preparing my bag to leave for the hospital. I called my mom and brother to let them know I was heading to the hospital. My contractions were getting really close together by this time and I could hardly take it.

I arrived at the hospital at 8:45 AM, I walked into the emergency room with about 10 people with me. Everyone in the emergency room stared at me as if they had never seen a pregnant girl before. The nurse at the counter took all my information and told me to have a seat and wait a while. I waited for about 10 minutes when a male nurse came with a wheelchair and rolled me into the OB room. I was in the observation room for about an hour when another nurse told me to walk around since I was still only 3 cm dilated. I took a walk for about 30 minutes when I couldn't take the pain anymore. When I returned to my room to lie down the nurse checked me, and I was now 4 cm. It was now time to prepare myself for delivery. I had initially decided not to have an epidural, but I could not take the pain. She checked how far I had dilated, and I was now 5cm. An hour later a group of nurses came in to give me the epidural. At about 9 PM my nurse came in and asked if my water had broken and I said no, not that I know of. She checked and she couldn't find the amniotic bag. She asked me if I was sure, and I said yes. She moved the baby's head around and sure enough, the water came rushing out. That little stain that I had seen earlier was my water.

After that everything just seemed to go by fast. At around 5 AM the nurse checked how much I had dilated, and I was 9cm. She told me that by 6 AM I would be pushing. I called and texted everyone and by 6 o'clock I was pushing. At this time the doctor turned off my dose of epidural since I couldn't feel the contractions. I pushed a lot of times and nothing. My baby would go down and when the contraction and pushing were over, she would move back up. It was a struggle, so the doctor used the suction cup twice before finally giving up on it. It popped off both times and she didn't want to hurt the baby. The doctor finally decided to cut me, which was called an episiotomy. Finally, my baby girl decided to join us. She cried once and then stopped. She was pale and her fingernails were black. She had stopped breathing, but in less than 20 seconds her doctor gave her oxygen and pumped her little chest with two fingers, her color returned, and she was breathing again. She was calm, and when they brought her to me, I kissed her forehead, and she made a little noise. I will never forget that noise. I loved her the very moment she came out. She weighed 7 pounds 11 ounces and was 21 inches long.

Now she is 4 months old and is a very happy little baby. She laughs and coos and gives you little stares. She is everything to me and I am very happy that I decided to keep her. No, it wasn't a good time to bring her into this world, but it happened.

I sometimes think about my young life and feel that if I could go back in time I would do things differently, especially the one to wait until marriage to have sex. I don't regret having my wonderful little girl, but I just wish I would have waited a little longer.

—Julie G.

EXERCISE 4.1 MOTHER-DAUGHTER ACTIVITIES

Find the terms related to reproduction in the word maze below.

```
E  W  S  L  Q  T  X  N  M  J  X  H  M  I  C  E  S  H  E  M  M  Z
T  B  I  P  H  M  B  P  L  C  F  O  H  B  H  G  I  L  P  U  E  D
I  S  U  T  E  V  L  O  X  W  D  L  Y  X  R  A  Y  H  I  I  N  J
X  E  E  T  H  R  A  Z  J  N  T  H  E  Q  O  I  T  E  D  R  S  X
P  T  V  I  N  D  M  S  O  O  N  M  H  H  M  R  S  E  I  T  T  P
I  S  W  D  U  A  R  C  D  Y  V  B  S  H  O  R  O  P  D  E  U  K
D  E  S  G  G  E  I  A  W  E  K  Q  R  V  S  A  V  H  Y  M  A  A
Q  T  V  T  J  P  D  P  W  R  F  I  U  T  O  C  U  P  M  O  T  P
A  Z  D  S  W  F  P  X  O  A  Q  E  Y  D  M  S  L  E  I  D  I  L
B  T  U  O  G  W  U  V  V  L  L  Z  R  Z  E  I  A  W  S  N  O  W
P  D  Q  H  O  E  H  K  G  Z  L  V  Q  N  S  M  T  F  L  E  N  O
Y  T  I  L  I  T  R  E  F  N  I  A  H  X  S  O  I  E  C  W  V  Y
O  M  H  I  X  L  R  L  W  V  F  G  F  E  B  L  O  X  Q  A  A  R
E  D  B  H  J  U  U  I  V  V  E  O  M  C  Y  K  N  N  R  K  Y  A
E  G  O  E  Z  J  S  E  S  N  U  R  E  T  H  R  A  I  D  D  U  I
A  B  O  R  T  I  O  N  E  W  W  U  T  N  M  D  E  D  J  G  C  T
G  N  O  I  T  A  G  I  L  L  A  B  U  T  S  S  U  X  O  S  M  E
```

ABORTION	CHROMOSOMES	CONDOM
EGGS	ENDOMETRIUM	EPIDIDYMIS
FALLOPIANTUBE	GENE	INFERTILITY
IUD	MENSTRUATION	MISCARRIAGE
OVARIES	OVULATION	SPERM
TESTES	TUBAL LIGATION	URETHRA
VASDEFERNS	WITHDRAWAL	

Using the terms from the "word maze", complete the statements about family planning by filling in the blanks.

1. The _____ traps the sperm and keeps them from entering the vagina.

2. Next to each testis is a coil tube called the _____.

3. The _____ or intrauterine device, is a small, soft plastic or metal device which is inserted into the uterus.

4. _____ refers to the removal of the penis from the vagina before ejaculation.

5. _____ is the temporary condition of being unable to conceive.

6. _____ is sometimes called spontaneous abortion.

7. This bloody discharge leaves the body through the vagina in the process called _____.

8. A woman is born with 400 immature egg cells that are stored in her two _____.

9. A _____ is the basic unit of heredity.

10. The inner lining of the uterus is called the _____.

11. The two ejaculatory ducts are located side by side and connect to the _____.

12. Sperm is carried through the _____ _____.

13. _____ _____ is the surgical procedure for sterilization of a woman.

14. After leaving the ovary, the egg passes into one of two tubes called the _____ _____.

15. _____ is the removal of a fetus from the uterus before development is complete.

16. The parent gives the unborn child 23 _____.

17. In reproduction there are two sex cells, the _____ from the male and the _____ from the female.

18. A woman's role in reproduction is to provide _____.

19. Sperm are produced in a man's two _____ or testicles.

20. An egg is released from the ovaries through the process called _____.

SEGMENT V

FOLLOW THE LEAD

Objective:

the mother will...
Teach her daughter to accept and understand the importance of responsibility.

Perpetrador

So, you still don't understand it yet, do you?
Life, this thing you're involved in since birth.

Yes, you're afraid of life, aren't you?
Look at you, yes you are, I can see it and smell your fear.
To fear life is to fear you.
Fear is the mind-killer,
Your fear, like which you are, is ever-changing.
Every moment of awareness is an ever-changing trepidation.

To understand you is to understand life.
First, you must be successful at them both.

—Airrass AogAod

ESTABLISHING ROUTINES AND COMMUNICATION

ESTABLISHING ROUTINES FOR THE house, work great when your daughter knows what is expected of her. During the week, creating a routine for keeping household chores maintained, when homework is to be done, preparing for the next day, having dinner on the table, and being ready for bed by a specific time are important tools to teach your daughter. Oh, yes, don't forget family time. At the dinner table asking about school, friends, and boys is a great way to strike up a conversation. Allowing your daughter to do most of the talking and surprisingly you will be amazed how much you will learn. Also, include your day of activities to keep her informed about what you are doing as well.

At random times, visit your daughter in her room. Call it her apartment and when you visit, knock on the door before you enter allowing her to tell you to come in. This shows her that you respect her privacy just as you expect her to respect yours. When visiting, make this time for girls to talk, making actively listening a priority as it is an important part of communication.

Acting as the listener, listen with your eyes and ears which will convey to your daughter that you are listening. Understanding that active listening involves more than hearing what she is saying but will encourage her to share makes her feel she is being respected and accepted. You are listening with undivided attention will also help her to clarify the meaning of her message and minimize the chance for misinterpretation of her ideas.

Look at this chart to get an idea of being an active listener

An active listener will:	Description
Pay attention	Stop what you are doing and give full attention
Acknowledge what is being said	Nod your head, say "I see" or something to indicate that you are listening. Repeat simple phrases to show you are listening and that you understood.
Let your daughter do most of the talking	Make occasional comments or ask a few questions.
Acknowledge her feelings	Show that you are compassionate about what is being said.

Don't Set Negative Barriers to Open Communication

WHEN KEEPING A LINE of communication open with your daughter, you may want to proceed slowly when ordering, directing, demanding, warning, and threatening when giving instructions. Take precautions when judging, lecturing, giving solutions, criticizing, blaming, and advising. Try to avoid the red zone. These areas can cause a total breakdown in communication if you ridicule, name-calling, assume, analyze, or question most situations.

Keeping an open line of communication will keep a positive flow of things in your household and will make your daughter feel that she is a part of the structure of how your house is managed. It is important for you, the mother to demonstrate household management. You are the leader, so for your followers to follow, show that you have studied your route, marking it from start to finish. This will send the message that you are responsible and will teach your daughter to do the same.

Taking Responsibility

TEACHING YOUR DAUGHTER TO accept responsibility begins with accepting your own responsibility. Taking responsibility for the choices you make, the actions in which you take, and the direction of your path to success is the most powerful foundation principle you will embrace. You are completely responsible for your life. Not allowing others to lead you around is how your daughter will view your leadership qualities. The most important aspect of taking responsibility for your life is to acknowledge that your life is your responsibility. You are in charge. Complete the parent responsibility contract on the next page to confirm your leadership skills and promise to yourself to share with your daughter.

Now, that you have outlined your requirements as a parent, together with your daughter, create a contract that she can build from understanding what is expected of her as a growing and maturing young lady. Look at the form following the Parent Responsibility Contract as a model.

EXERCISE 5.1: PARENT RESPONSIBILITY CONTRACT

I _____, do solemnly promise to act as a responsible parent

        Your Name

to my daughter _____. I will meet the following expectations with

        Daughter's Name

regards to my parental responsibilities.

- I promise to provide food, shelter, and clothing.
- I will provide medical care when you are sick.
- I will correct my daughter's misbehavior as a teaching tool and not criticize or
- ridicule her.
- I will demonstrate to my daughter acceptable morals and values.
- I will provide and display to my daughter self-esteem needs.
- I will assist in my daughter's decision-making when asked.
- I will correct my daughter using corrective criticism.
- I will provide my daughter with a safe environment.
- I will provide my daughter with basic needs.
- I will teach my daughter mutual respect.
- I will provide to my daughter with structured, consistent, predictable, and fair discipline.
- I will support my daughter's educational requirements.
- I will create a bond with my daughter to fulfill a parent/child friendship.
- I promise to teach my daughter good leadership skills.
- I promise to listen to my daughter without interruptions and judging.

It is my greatest desire to fulfill the above obligations stated in this contract. I do realize that by writing these obligations alone will not make me a quality parent, but to work diligently each day will allow me a goal to reaching my best.

_____   _____

      Mother's Signature   Date

Here are a few terms related to teenage concerns that may help when your daughter begins to identify the information, she will include in her Daughter's Requirement Contract.

Abstinence	Grades
Boyfriends	High School
Curfew	Sleepovers
Dating	Prom
Friend Girls	College
Privacy	Cars
Respect	Safety
Sex	Working

EXERCISE 5.2: DAUGHTER'S RESPONSIBILITY CONTRACT

I _____, do solemnly promise to act as a responsible

      Daughter's Name

daughter while under the supervision of _____. I will meet the following

                          Guardian

expectations with regards to my responsibilities as a growing and maturing young lady.

- I will _____

EXERCISE 5.3: TAKING RESPONSIBILITY WORD SEARCH

Search for words related to responsibility, then find the hidden word in your search.

```
A  B  S  T  I  N  E  N  C  E  R  E  S  P  O
G  N  M  S  I  B  I  Y  L  I  T  Y  Z  U  Y
N  R  X  O  K  S  C  Q  P  W  E  W  I  Z  L
I  Q  A  S  R  A  Z  T  C  E  P  S  E  R  Y
T  J  N  D  V  P  E  K  S  S  G  Q  E  T  K
A  F  R  I  E  N  D  G  I  R  L  S  E  C  I
D  B  R  W  L  S  Y  E  C  H  V  F  I  A  I
B  P  U  D  E  X  G  Y  D  T  A  O  R  R  E
D  E  T  P  J  H  I  J  V  S  S  X  O  S  W
U  U  C  B  O  Y  F  R  I  E  N  D  S  O  X
L  O  O  H  C  S  H  G  I  H  C  X  R  P  Z
N  S  L  E  E  P  O  V  E  R  S  K  B  K  G
E  G  E  L  L  O  C  S  Y  L  I  L  N  D  Y
W  E  F  R  U  C  G  U  E  N  P  Z  Z  A  S
N  V  K  E  Q  H  V  N  G  X  R  D  R  D  P
```

ABSTINENCE	BOYFRIENDS	CARS
COLLEGE	CURFEW	DATING
FRIENDGIRLS	GRADES	HIGHSCHOOL
PRIVACY	PROM	RESPECT
SAFETY	SEX	SLEEPOVERS
WORKING		

Preparation

+

Opportunity

=

Success

A GIFT FROM GOD

ALTHOUGH I AM A teenager; I feel that my life has been really hard. There have been a lot of problems in my family with the biggest problem being money.

In my house, my dad was the only one working. He works for a construction company, so, if it should rain, he doesn't work.

Last year I turned 15 and really wanted a quinceanera. My Mom said, "If I had one it would be a small dinner at my house, but my dad wanted me to have a party."

Just like any other girl of my culture, my dream was to have the full ceremony. My brother began working, to help my dad. Then, my dad was able to get a loan and with that money, they gave me my quinceanera. I will never forget what my parents did for me.

—Mariah

SEGMENT VI

MY FIRST TEACHER

Objective:

the mother will...
Understand the concern of teachers who chose
education as their career.

EDUCATION

IS THE

POWER Behind

SUCCESS

REFLECTIONS

AS A CHILD GROWING up in a rural area with four younger siblings, I used reading as a means of escape and entertainment. My love for reading was stimulated by my fourth-grade teacher, Miss Scott. As a student in her class, I admired her because she was totally committed to developing "passionate learners". No matter how many times or different ways she had to explain a concept, her patience and dedication with the slowest student was amazing. Having such a positive experience in her classroom made me want to become a teacher. Moreover, her style was the basis on which I would build my own philosophy of teaching and nourishing the learning environment in my own classroom.

Forty-one years ago, as I began my teaching career in a segregated high school in Hot Springs, Arkansas. As I entered the classroom as a first-year teacher, I was excited because I was following my passion. The students were all excited about coming to school and wanted to learn so they could go to college. I was reminded of my own vital role every time I witnessed a student's excitement or enthusiasm, particularly one who had not been previously motivated. At that point, I knew why Miss Scott never gave up on us; she was waiting for that spark in our eyes to become visible. The camaraderie among fellow teachers and administration was like family and this made teaching even more enjoyable.

Teaching, unlike in my earlier years, is more challenging than I'd like to endure. When I tell people that I have been teaching for forty-one years, the first question they asked is "How are students different from when you first started teaching?" Unfortunately, I have to say that students today are very different than students were in the past. What I have experienced in these last ten or twelve years is that students today have much more baggage to deal with in comparison to what students faced forty-one years ago.

When I first started teaching, students were not faced with decisions and distractions such as where they are going to live, where will they get that next meal or having to raise siblings. For example, years ago there were very few single parents, but strong two parent families, who were very involved in their children's education even though the parents, themselves, did not have an education. Sure, if a student had a discipline issue the child did not want the parents to be contacted, because they knew that if they got in trouble at school, they would get in trouble upon returning home. Parents taught their children morals, values and to respect all adults. Parents stressed getting an education and making good grades as a key to success.

On the other hand, since there are more single parent homes, the parents seem to leave it up to the students to be responsible, while the parents are working. It has been my experience that when students get in trouble today, the parents want to know what the teacher did to their children. It is my opinion, that many students today are not focused on learning, but are more concerned with wearing the latest styles of clothing and tennis shoes rather than playing sports, cheerleading, and drill team. Parents of today's students seem to be more concerned with their children walking across the stage for graduation and not how much they have learned.

—*Ella Jefferson*, Teacher
Alief ISD

THE EDUCATOR

What it really means to become a teacher

"Patience"

AN EFFORT TO UNDERSTAND

BECAME A TEACHER BECAUSE I wanted to pass knowledge to children. I became a high school teacher because I think the teen years are an exciting time of transition between childhood and adulthood. I knew there would be some discipline problems, but I never anticipated insurrection.

I did not realize that my background would be so different from that of the young adults I would teach. Also, my age has made a difference. When I went to school, challenging a teacher was unacceptable behavior and not to be even explored as an option. My parents and those of my friends taught us that, not only was school the most important thing we could do but also the teacher was always right; therefore, a call from the teacher was an extremely painful experience for us.

What I have experienced in teaching is students who come to the classroom with an attitude that the teacher is against them, the teacher must be challenged, and the teacher must win the encounter or is not to be respected. I now understand the rules, but I still do not understand their origin. Teaching is not how well you know your subject or how interesting you can make it. Before you can get to that, you must go through a type of initiation. If you fail, your expertise as an imparter of knowledge will not matter.

I have had great difficulty in reaching some of my minority students. I do not understand the attitude or the motivation behind it. I can only operate from my observations since my attempts at talking with the students with whom I have trouble, are met with a stone wall of insolent silence. This is not all students; people are individuals and I have managed to reach some whom I thought were hard and cold, only to find their problems were beyond my capacity to help. I did find that if I could get past the barrier they put up, they were warm, generous, wonderful people inside.

I realize that teachers are also individuals and that the experience some of my students have had before I get them has been negative. Some of the experiences my students have had with me have been negative, not because either of us wants them to be, but because we come to each other with such an abysmal gap in our understanding of each other.

Teachers need to be trained in what to expect. I had extensive training in curriculum, subject, and even classroom management, but none in understanding where these students are emotional. Classroom management does not address differences in culture, expectations, and attitude.

You said that white teachers were afraid of their black students. I have examined that statement and find that it is true in this respect - we fear what we do not understand. As I think back to my first days of teaching, I remember that my first emotion was a bewilderment and then the fear set in. I did not know what to do and I felt inadequate. Since those days I have run the gamut from bewilderment to fear to resentment to despair to determination. If I had not gotten to determination, quitting would have been the only choice and many teachers choose it. Some go on teaching, but they have quit caring. Determination, however, takes a toll in exhaustion and does not address the underlying problem.

I have been as honest as I can be, but as I read over this, I see I am still bewildered. I feel I have failed as a teacher, not because I am not well-founded in my subject, but because I have been unable to reach students who so desperately need the knowledge I have. Can you help me and other teachers who do not understand?

—Kathy

A child's love
for a parent

GROWING UP IS HARD TO DO

THERE HAVE BEEN MANY experiences that I have had over the course of my adolescence that I look back on and I realize how right my parents were in many situations. The most significant lessons I have learned have been a result of making mistakes with the opposite sex and life lessons in general. I remember my mother always telling me that I have the rest of my life to be an adult and do my own thing, but it really didn't register until recently as I have gotten older and graduated from college. I remember when I thought I was in love at the tender age of 16, and I was disobedient and dated a guy that didn't have my best interest at heart. I wasn't allowed to see him or talk to him, and I was very bitter and mad because I felt I was really in love and couldn't live without this guy.

If I had known then, what I know now, it would have saved my family and me a lot of headaches. I was insistent on learning my own lessons and doing what I thought was best for me at the time. Although I am only 21 and still young, I have grown more, and I now realize that what my parents were trying to get through to me was that I had the rest of my life to be "grown" and now that I am getting there, I wish I could go back.

They only want the best for me, and they gave me advice because they want to see me succeed and protect me from the dangers in the world. I also look at things differently now because they have dedicated their whole lives to see me happy and providing for my brothers and me, and I feel like I owe it to them to listen to what they say and make them proud.

My brothers are 16 and 17, and I try to talk to them, and I can see how hard it is to try to tell a kid something beneficial for their lives and they don't listen. I can only hope and pray that my kids will listen to me more than I listened to my parents, and they will see that I speak only from experience and that I want the best for them.

I believe I am a quality person now only because my mother talked to me constantly until she was blue in the face about making the right decisions and keeping God first. I think that she didn't give up on me is the reason why I know I will be a success in my life. I would encourage every parent to not give up on their child and continue to preach and talk to them even when it seems like there is no hope and there's nothing left to say.

Love,

Allison

What Happened To

"it Takes a Village"

—African Proverb

OBSTACLES

I BEGAN WORKING IN AN inner-city high school as a Coach and Substance Abuse Monitor. I have found that kids of today have a lot of obstacles to overcome, with the increase in single-parent homes, drugs, incarceration, and the simple lack of interest in a student's well-being at school.

Kids want to learn and better themselves, but they have no voice or positive role models at home. I'm not saying this is the case in every household, but it is in the majority. We have mothers raising children alone, and sons who eventually become bigger than they are in size and start to intimidate them. Daughters who follow the daily routine of seeing their mothers date numerous men. As well as accepting abuse from both genders and being outright disrespectful to any authority figure.

My opinion is that the parents, schools, and the community need to find some common ground (and pledge to it) in the upbringing of every child. This will make things a little better for everyone (especially the child). IT DEFINITELY "TAKES A VILLAGE TO RAISE A CHILD," but all of this starts with the person in the mirror.

—Karl

As a high school student, I can remember my teacher saying.....

"You should never get up as early as we do,

stay all day at a learning institution, then, leave at

the end of the day and not know any more than

you knew when you awaken that morning."

—Gwen Gistarb

DISAPPOINTMENT

AS AN EDUCATOR AND parent, I have found the gravest disappointment to be the lack of parental participation, especially among the African American and Hispanic populations. I am a teacher in an area that is predominately Black and Hispanic-populated. The students are in such great need of guidance and participation in the parent's art, but they almost never seem to receive it. It is typical for a child to fail an entire semester, a year even, and we never get any type of response from a parent until it is too late. I understand that in underprivileged economic areas most parents are working more than one job to compensate for the poor salary they receive due to their own lack of education. Or the situation may be that some of the students come from single-parent families where the parent's presence is less important than that parent being able to provide for their families. However, as parents, we must realize that our primary, number one responsibility is to our children. Yes, as educators we spend the most time with someone else's children during the day, and we do our best to educate them during this time. But the nurturing, counseling, and guidance that the children so desperately need, must come from the parent.

—S. Williams

THE SUCCESSFUL PARENT
AS A TEACHER

MOTHERS ARE THEIR DAUGHTERS' first teachers. When taking on this role, there are some common characteristics that you will share with educators. Here are a few keys to becoming a successful teacher. As in most facets of life, being a good parent and/or teacher depends on your attitude and your patience. Having the following qualities will help you when you begin to teach.

- Considerate of Feelings
- Consistency
- Dedication
- Fairness
- Flexibility
- Leadership skills
- Positive Attitude
- Respectful
- Rules
- Sense of Caring
- Sense of Humor
- Structure
- Supportive
- Trust
- Understanding

EXERCISE 6.1: PARENT AS A TEACHER WORD SEARCH

```
L  O  S  V  E  Y  K  S  C  K  B  M  I  D  U  V  F  H  F  R
F  Y  R  S  O  Q  H  K  E  O  M  T  O  X  C  T  H  O  L  O
W  L  G  U  E  B  N  J  R  N  N  Z  H  T  R  U  P  A  E  M
R  L  U  Z  F  N  X  L  H  P  S  S  O  R  S  A  W  F  X  U
Z  W  S  W  R  B  R  O  J  K  I  E  I  N  H  I  W  L  I  H
J  B  F  V  Z  C  Q  I  I  F  D  K  O  S  M  S  B  O  B  F
K  C  U  X  A  O  Q  D  A  O  Q  R  I  F  T  Z  J  U  I  O
S  C  M  I  N  N  D  T  E  F  E  S  V  W  C  E  V  V  L  E
N  D  D  P  B  X  S  M  E  R  J  U  N  X  A  A  N  A  I  S
E  D  U  T  I  T  T  A  E  V  I  T  I  S  O  P  R  C  T  N
O  V  J  A  O  F  F  P  U  W  Q  L  B  D  U  V  D  I  Y  E
O  C  X  J  T  U  Z  U  V  D  S  T  N  E  Y  Z  V  M  N  S
E  V  I  T  R  O  P  P  U  S  R  G  N  D  B  Q  U  G  E  G
N  R  E  S  P  E  C  T  F  U  L  S  E  I  P  B  X  E  V  U
T  X  K  B  Z  M  E  P  S  D  X  L  L  C  Z  K  U  X  I  G
W  A  Z  N  R  A  A  T  M  T  F  K  X  A  A  Z  P  Y  N  I
U  N  D  E  R  S  T  A  N  D  I  N  G  T  R  V  O  C  P  J
H  F  R  E  C  L  J  L  Q  V  F  Y  A  I  I  I  F  Z  O  O
W  T  W  R  P  X  U  Y  U  K  M  V  Y  O  A  N  B  C  B  F
W  L  E  R  N  K  L  O  B  T  Z  T  L  N  Z  H  P  M  H  M
```

CONSISTENCY	DEDICATION	FAIRNESS
FLEXIBILITY	POSITIVE ATTITUDE	RESPECTFUL
SENSEOFCARING	SENSE OF HUMOR	SUPPORTIVE
TRUST	UNDERSTANDING	CONSIDERATE OF FEELINGS

When life serves you a bowl of Lemons,

What will You do with them?

Segment VII

Because I Am, You Will Be

Objective:

the mother will...
Display character building traits
when raising her daughter(s).

CHARACTER BUILDING

What is character?

A person who demonstrates being a good person, someone to look up to based on society's expectations. Set a good example of someone who knows right from wrong. Character is how one wants others to see who they are as a person.

Why is character important?

The importance of building good character begins from birth when parents begin to teach morals, respect, correcting attitudes, and demonstrating good leadership. Learning to be good to oneself and to others will show self-respect. Setting an example for others to follow and being inspirational for those who want to tread on the righteous path.

What are the Important Factors of Character?

- **Trustworthiness** – Always practice honesty and reliability.
- **Respect** - Treat others as you would like to be treated.
- **Responsibility** - Do what you are supposed to do.
- **Fairness** - Play by the rules.
- **Caring** - Be kind and compassionate.
- **Citizenship** – Obey the laws and do your share to make your school and community better.

SELF DETERMINATION

The quality of one's character includes the following self-determined qualities individuals strive to build within themselves.

- Attitude
- Awareness
- Caring
- Citizenship
- Commitment
- Communication
- Confidence
- Consideration
- Cooperation
- Courage
- Courtesy
- Creativity
- Diligence
- Discipline
- Discretion
- Endurance
- Enthusiasm
- Fairness
- Faith

- Focus
- Generosity
- Honesty
- Humility
- Initiative
- Integrity
- Kindness
- Leadership
- Loyalty
- Motivation
- Patience
- Punctuation
- Resourcefulness
- Respect
- Responsibility
- Self-Control
- Sincerity
- Tolerance
- Trustworthiness

EXERCISE 7.1: CHARACTER TRAIT ACTIVITY

Choose from the list of character traits you live by, then, give an accountability of the last time you represented one or more.

Character Trait	Accountability

The Don't of Character Building

- Bad Attitude
- Blame others for your mistakes
- Change a story
- Cheat
- Do anything wrong
- Include others in your dishonesty
- Insensitive
- Judgmental
- Lie
- Lose confidence when you fail
- Make excuses for your wrongdoing
- Manipulate others
- Point the finger at others
- Put down other people
- Rudeness
- Sneakiness
- Spread gossip
- Steal
- Take more than your share
- Use insults to embarrass others
- Use threats

EXERCISE 7.2: CHARACTER-BUILDING SKILLS WORD SEARCH

Identify words that will assist in learning character building.

```
U  Y  U  E  C  N  A  R  E  L  O  T  I  E  P
Y  T  I  L  I  V  I  C  C  Q  W  R  N  C  A
S  S  E  N  D  N  I  K  A  O  Y  O  T  N  T
F  A  I  R  N  E  S  S  Y  U  N  N  E  E  I
O  Y  S  E  T  R  U  O  C  Y  P  O  G  G  E
C  O  N  V  I  C  T  I  O  N  S  H  R  I  N
T  O  G  E  T  H  E  R  N  E  S  S  I  L  C
H  E  L  P  F  U  L  N  E  S  S  Y  T  I  E
N  O  I  T  A  R  E  P  O  O  C  U  Y  D  V
T  R  U  S  T  W  O  R  T  H  I  N  E  S  S
G  C  G  P  I  H  S  N  E  Z  I  T  I  C  E
S  E  L  F  C  O  N  T  R  O  L  A  N  F  C
P  E  R  S  E  R  V  E  R  A  N  C  E  O  A
G  E  N  E  R  O  S  I  T  Y  M  F  J  S  E
Y  T  I  L  I  B  I  S  N  O  P  S  E  R  P
```

CITIZENSHIP	CIVILITY	CONVICTIONS
COOPERATION	COURTESY	DILIGENCE
FAIRNESS	GENEROSITY	HELPFULNESS
HONOR	INTEGRITY	KINDNESS
PATIENCE	PEACE	PERSERVERANCE
RESPONSIBILITY	SELFCONTROL	TOGETHERNESS
TOLERANCE	TRUSTWORTHINESS	

EXERCISE 7.3: CHARACTER-BUILDING TERMS

Using the terms on the previous page, write a sentence for each demonstrating your knowledge and understanding.

1.

2.

3.

4.

5.

6.

7.

8.

9.

10.

11.

12.

13.

14.

15.

16.

17.

18.

19.

20.

EXERCISE 7.4: ESSAY ACTIVITY

Write a one-page essay describing your character and comparing it to the character of your daughter.

SEGMENT VIII

A MOTHER'S HEART

Objective:

the mother will... Demonstrate compassion toward the feelings of their children.

APOLOGY TO MY CHILDREN

I WAS YOUNG AND HAD lived my life without responsibilities. Nineteen, married with one child, then another, I forgot about my children's feelings before I separated and divorced their father. I did not realize the impact that it would have on them. Bouncing them back and forth between houses and trying to keep them grounded was difficult.

They seemed to have been fine at the time, but a few years later, after I began to grow up, I began to see their unhappiness. They never said anything, but when I would look at them, I could see deep in their eyes.

At the beginning of my so-called freedom (that is, without a husband) several years passed and I began to change. I started to feel lonely inside and would think a lot about what I had done by separating our little happy family. I thought the grass was greener on this side of freedom, but how wrong I was. I couldn't find stability in any relationship and now I was alone without anyone to worry about me.

As the years began to pass, I watched my children grow up and become stable in the lives they were building. I kept a very tight rein which is why we have the close relationship that we have today.

Now I am a grandmother with two wonderful grandchildren, and I have found happiness again seeing parts of my children in them. It's wonderful on this side of parenthood. After divorcing and raising my children many years later, I sit alone much of the time in a quiet house now sometimes wishing I had never initiated the change I forced in our lives. It is my wish that my children would accept my apology for disrupting their lives. Even though they endured the change of not having both parents in the same house, they remained grounded.

I love them both and hope in their lives they would not follow in my footsteps in marriage, but find peace when things are not going as they may have thought they should.

— A Mother's Love

Children should never leave home to *misrepresent* their parents.

WHEN MOTHERS DON'T TEACH

D O YOU REMEMBER THE quiet time you spent with yourself and your unborn daughter thinking of all the wonderful things you were going to teach her. For nine months all that you could think of was your little daughter and sharing with the proud daddy your plans for your baby's future. Shopping and preparing the baby's room for her arrival was the only thing important. How happy you were reading books to help you understand what to expect when that great day arose. Knowing that your little baby girl would arrive with her own personality; you planned to guide her to perfection, hoping that you would be successful in molding her to find her own.

Can you remember seeing a child acting poorly in a public place and you would say to yourself, "My child will not act that way because I will teach my baby to know right from wrong?" This type of thinking is part of a parent's continuous journey of using creative methods for teaching each of their children because they know each child is different. Being a parent is hard work. From the day of your baby's birth throughout her teenage years, self-discipline is taught, because your child must represent your teachings when they are without your supervision.

Sometimes your teachings may be without flaws, but your little lady will, for whatever reason, misrepresent what she has been taught. When it comes to acting inappropriately, the same things that she is trying now did not work for us in years past and they will not work for her today. Each generation thinks that they invented the things they are experiencing. They don't realize that we are called parents for a reason, just as our parents before us, because we know so much about life's hidden secrets.

Thinking back to my youth, I see one thing that is different from today: freedom of speech. Children have the need to defend themselves more so than we did and even further back than I can remember. Our parents did not allow us to speak as freely as today's younger generation. Many adults today still do not talk back to their parents, nor do they use any form of profanity. This is called respecting our elders. Not only did you not talk back to your parents, but you also did not talk back to any adult. If you did you knew what would happen when your parents found out.

Young people have misunderstood what freedom of speech means. Teaching your children tact can help them develop a better attitude. It's not what you say, it is how you say it. I can remember being punished for talking back to my mother. I always had to have the last word and this, of course, would get me grounded. Being grounded meant you would lose privileges plus any other punishment your parents would dream up when they are angry with you. This is something today's teens know nothing about. Discipline has changed tremendously, and some parents have confused it with abuse.

When I speak about discipline, I'm not talking about slapping your kids around. That is abuse. I'm not talking about cursing at your kids. That, too, is abuse. I'm not talking about having a knockdown, drag-out screaming session because that is, abuse also, nor am I talking about putting your kids out of the house. What I am talking about are rules.

Rules teach your children about attitude adjusting. When there are rules and they are enforced, then, there are no unanswered questions. Your job as a parent is to create the rules, and your children's job is to follow them. Creating, enforcing, and executing rules will allow your children to develop values that society will expect from them. These rules will not divide a family but will develop a stronger relationship to build on. Allowing parents and children not to only respect one another, but, also, to develop a friendship that will build a closer bond. Creating a structural household will allow your children to grow with the right and wrong of life and to know the difference. Then, when they have choices to make, they will understand the steps in the Decision-Making Process.

Teaching our children to think before speaking will teach them to make better choices in life. Learning to think before speaking will give them the opportunity to choose tactful words when communicating with you and others.

When my kids were growing up, my daughter had a bad attitude. She was mean to her brother so much that I was forever coming to his rescue. For years she was so mean to him that I would tell her that when he grows up and learns to defend himself, he would get her for all that she had done to him. She even tried this business with me, but quickly had to stop it. As they were getting older, it seemed as though she tried to hold everything over his head. She, of course, got a car first, and if he wanted to use it, she made him wash it before and after and refill the tank before returning it. Even though she loved her brother dearly, her mistreatment was the result of jealousy, which was understandable because she had been the only child and grandchild for three and a half years.

When my son was in the eleventh grade, he gave his sister a Christmas present, a beautifully wrapped gift box. She excitedly tore the paper open to find a brand-new shiny Phillip screwdriver. She did not understand the moral of the gift, and he told her that it was an attitude adjuster. It took him years, but he got her to change the way she talked to him and others, something I had tried for years to do.

Do we recognize our children's faults, or do we make excuses for them? If we guide our children to become more self-evaluating, then it will allow them to follow our lead in their behavior. It is important to teach our children that in order to respect others they must learn self-respect.

If we demonstrate our concerns about how we look at what happens in our lives and how we respond, our children will ultimately understand what defines a positive attitude. By doing so, then, our children will see the good side of any given situation and other people. Practicing a positive attitude in the home will influence the atmosphere in most places.

As parents we want our children to have the best that life will offer, and it is our responsibility to teach them that life is only what we make of it. If we teach them to love and respect us, then they will love and respect others. This is called discipline.

When a baby is born, we are to provide them with every ounce of whom they will become. Just as the poem "Can I Talk to You," states, they are only asking for your guidance and if not provided they will not only destroy themselves, but they will also destroy you as well. It is your responsibility to give them your very best. When doing so will make their journey to develop an easier and more pleasurable ride to adulthood. The need to shower them with motivational compliments too will help them to develop a secure feeling for themselves.

At the beginning of each school year, I give my students a motivational packet that has a rubber band, a button cover, a toothpick, a band-aid, a candy, a gold thread, an eraser, and a lifesaver. As I pass them to each student, I explain that each of the enclosed items has a special meaning. The rubber band symbolizes being able to expand and grow, the button cover reminds them to button their lips and listen, a toothpick to help pick through the good and bad qualities in all things, a band-aid to avoid band-aid solutions, a candy because everyone needs a reward, a piece of yarn to keep you all together, an eraser because everyone makes mistakes sometimes and that's ok and lastly a lifesaver as a reminder to always look for their earthly family for support.

Amari's Fish, Jack

⁓

AMARI'S FISH DIED AND he was very emotional. I explained that we are all spirits, including Jack. I told him that even though Jack was not here in his physical body, Jack would always be with him in Spirit. Amari tried to comfort himself with this wisdom, but I could tell he was still struggling with this concept; Spirit can exist in a physical body or outside a physical body.

The next morning as Amari was having breakfast, I noticed he wasn't eating, and his eyes were glazed over as he was about to cry. I went to comfort him and asked him to tell me why he was so upset. This is what he said, as he burst into tears, "I know that Jack's spirit is with me right now, but I miss his body!"

His words were so heartfelt and made me both laugh and cry at the same time. I guess this is how we all have felt at the loss of a loved one but just could not articulate it as honestly as Amari did.

—Daphne Wills, Amari's Mom

A Single Mom

IF YOU WOULD SET a temperature gauge in your home, what would it read? Cloudy, partly cloudy, rainy, stormy, or is the sun shining? Periodically, check the temperature in your homes just in case a storm is in the forecast. Quietly watching our daughter's every move, being responsible for creating an atmosphere that is conducive to everyone's needs, and setting a pace that is acceptable to the requirements of what is called a structured home.

Whether or not it is a nuclear household or a single-parent dwelling, the rules are still the same. Juggling our roles for a successfully run house can be questionable when you as the parent are being given a test and having to grade it too. Sometimes mistakes will be made but knowing those mistakes and immediately correcting them will allow us the possibility of passing with flying colors.

Being a nuclear family is sometimes just as hard as being a single-parent family. Surely, a single-parent family has a much more difficult task than that a nuclear one, of course, but single-parent families can be just as effective when the rules are etched in stone from the beginning of parenthood.

Many times, I've heard that when children begin to get into trouble it seems that society wants to blame it on the absentee father. Many times, this is true, but only if the mother has not enforced the house rules. I use an example of the mother more so than the father being the single parent because statistically, it is more likely that the mother is left to raise her children.

I believe that if a single mother strongly navigates her path and is sure of her destination, then, her children will follow. But, if she acts unsure of her direction or which route, she plans to take, her children will test their own paths and seek what they perceive is better. Children need you to lead the way and when you seem to not know which way to travel, they may take the wrong side of the fork in the road. So as parents we must determine our destinies so that our daughters will have a chance to become upstanding citizens.

EXERCISE 8.1: WORDS WITH COMPASSION

Study the following compassionate words, then, include a few of your own.

Happiness	Interested	Affectionate	Eagerness	Fearless
calm	fascinated	tender	earnest	encouraged
satisfied	intrigued	soft	aggressive	daring
comfortable	inquiring	desirous	avid	confident
joyous	excited	warm	zealous	brave
ecstatic	curious	loving	intent	heroic
enthusiastic	absorbed	seductive	anxious	determined
inspired	engrossed	close	keen	secure
grateful	concerned	passionate	hyper	independent
peaceful	sincere	open		reassured
spirited	inquisitive	sexy		courageous
New Words	**New Words**	**New Words**	**New Words**	**New Words**

EXERCISE 8.2: DESCRIBE YOUR HEART

Now use the words on the previous page to describe your heart.

My heart is...

Welcome to the Real World

Segment IX

Reaching Your Highest Level

Objective:

the mother will...
Identify the important tools that are required for setting
lifestyle goals and preparing for success.

FACING THE WORLD ON MY OWN

Alone and left on my own, I struggle to survive.
Only my hard work I would condone,
because of those against me who would connive.
Those long summer days
slowly turned to Fall.
Out with the stressful haze,
and in with my duties on call.
This began my senior year,
for the first time solo.
But at last, it was finally here
for me to face alone.
Although the last year has been tough,
I cannot dismiss life.
At last, I've finally made it here,
Alone, but strong enough to overcome the strife I've left behind.

—Sandi Canady

GOAL SETTING

I T IS IMPORTANT TO know the meaning of setting goals. Knowing that life goals are the way you want to spend your time and energy in the future. What you want to achieve. When thinking about the type of lifestyle you would like to have someday, set goals.

Fold a sheet of paper lengthwise, then write short-term on one side and long-term on the other. You will then begin to sort your goals to reduce the stress of determining where your life will end. Ask yourself the following questions:

- Do I feel that school is important?
- Will school prepare the foundation for my future?
- What do I want to accomplish in life?
- Do I want to get married?
- Do I want to raise a family?
- Do I want a high income or just enough money to be comfortable?
- Where would I like to live?
- What kind of house will I buy?
- What excites me?
- What do I want out of life?
- What are my skills?
- What have I learned so far?
- Will I be successful without an education?
- What is important to me?

Now imagine your life a few years from today. Can you see yourself in a different place than before you mapped out your future? Sketch out the way you'd like to live. Look a little closer at yourself to see if your career choice would be a realistic one. On the next page, you will determine your aptitude by using the aptitude scale. Look up aptitude tests on the internet for further testing your skills and abilities.

WHAT IS APTITUDE?

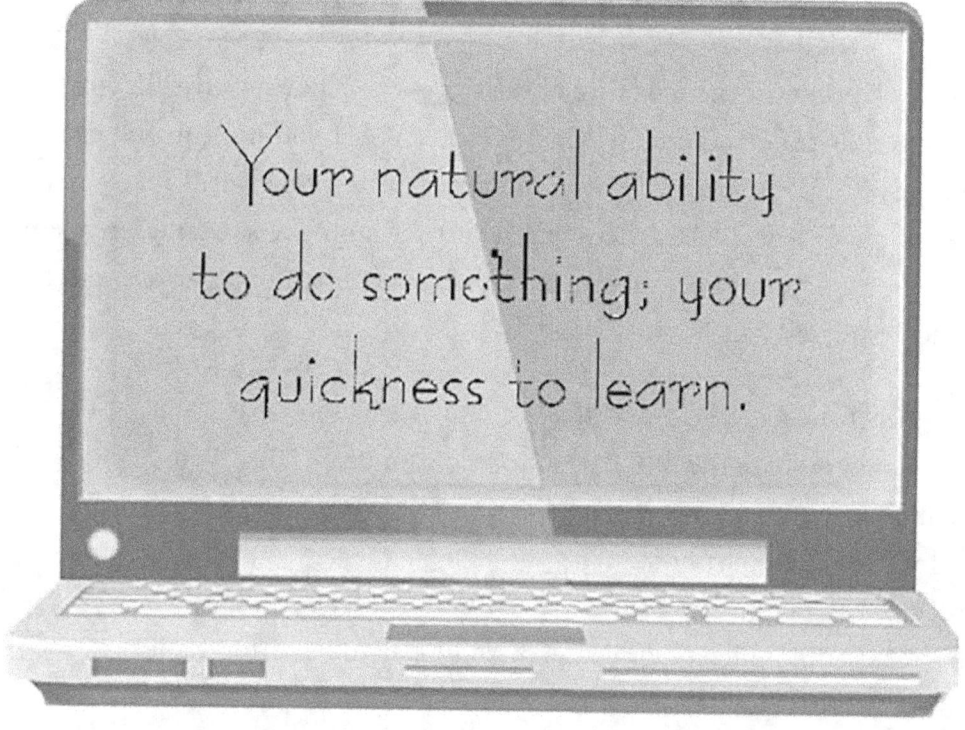

Your natural ability to do something; your quickness to learn.

THE APTITUDE SCALE

EXERCISE 9.1: IDENTIFY YOUR APTITUDE

1. Intelligence	General learning ability: the ability to catch on easily.
2. Verbal	The ability to present information or ideas clearly and effectively.
3. Numerical	The ability to perform mathematical skills quickly and accurately.
4. Spatial	The ability to understand forms in space and understand relationships of plane and solid objects.
5. Form Perception	The ability to make comparisons and to see slight differences in shapes and shadings of figures and widths and lengths of lines.
6. Clerical Perception	The ability to observe differences in copy or to proofread words and numbers.
7. Finger Dexterity	The ability to move the fingers rapidly and accurately manipulate small objects with the fingers.
8. Manual Dexterity	The ability to work with the hands in placing and turning motions.
9. Motor Coordination	The ability to make a movement accurately and quickly.

From the list above, choose skills that best fit your aptitude. Then, from this list determine what you may decide as your career focus.

1.

2.

3.

4.

5.

Place your choice here: _____

Now, you have chosen your best aptitude. From here you will be able to determine which type of education is needed to prepare you for a lifelong career.

EXERCISE 9.2: YOUR VALUES

What are your values? Identify your values by using the chart below. Include your own interests to justify each of your values.

Values	Interest
1. Career	
2. Financial Security	
3. Job Security	
4. Prestigious Position	
5. Defining Skilled Qualities	
6. Creating Independence	
7. Management	
8. People Person	
9. Variety of Interest	
10. Problem Solving	

EXERCISE 9.3: YOUR PERSONAL INVENTORY

This form will help you determine how you might work better in some job areas better than others. Review the statements below. Then, check the ones that best describe you. For example: If you marked most of the time on using a computer and liking to work alone, a clerical job might suit you, but if you said you can tell other people what to do and control your temper, a management job could be right up your alley.

	Most of time	Sometimes	Never
I can use a computer.			
I can operate electronic equipment.			
I can get to work on time.			
I am dependable.			
I can follow directions.			
I can tell other people what to do.			
I don't like to make changes.			
I do what I say I can do.			
I am honest.			
I would rather work alone.			
I would rather work with others.			
I am patient.			
I like others to value my work.			
I am loyal to people.			
I can accept corrective criticism.			
I am reliable.			
I am a dedicated worker.			
I can control my temper.			

EXERCISE 9.4: YOUR GOALS

What are your goals?

Use the space below to make a map of how you plan to reach your goals.

SEGMENT IX

WHAT YOU SHOULD KNOW ABOUT EMPLOYERS

The saying, "First Impressions are Lasting Impressions" is important when prospective employers are looking to hire an applicant. Although an applicant might be qualified, some of the reasons employers may or may not hire her are as follows.

- Poor personal appearance and/or hygiene
- "Know-it-all" attitude
- No purpose or career goals
- Lack of interest or enthusiasm
- Lack of confidence and poise
- Discussion of the salary too soon
- Highest level of education is a GED (General Equivalency Diploma)
- Excuse-maker
- Lack of courtesy
- Criticism of past employer
- No eye contact
- Weak handshake
- Lack of knowledge of the company
- Late to an interview with or without explanation
- No questions about the job
- Not wanting to start at the bottom
- No direct answers to questions
- Short-term commitment to the company

THINGS EMPLOYERS DON'T LIKE EMPLOYEES TO DO

- Lie on your resume
- Are late to work (tardiness), miss work frequently, or leave early regularly
- Sexually harass a co-worker
- Have a lack of customer service
- Use company funds (expense account/credit cards)

- Socialize too much
- Gossip
- Perform the minimum amount of work required (Just getting by)
- Not taking responsibility for mistakes (pointing the finger)
- Misrepresent the company
- Make your boss look bad
- Fail to live up to a job commitment
- Start Problems
- Handle business outside of your department (giving wrong information)
- Do not follow the dress code

QUALITIES EMPLOYERS LIKE IN AN EMPLOYEE

Some employers like to see certain basic positive qualities in their employees. Many others will depend on the company climate as well as the individual likes and dislikes of the chief executive officer, management, and supervisors. These likes can include the following characteristics:

- Enthusiasm
- Dependability
- Initiative
- Ability to work on a team
- Company dress codes
- Ability to follow policies and procedures

WRITING RESUMES

A resume is a portrait of who you are. This written summary will include your employment, objectives, work experience, education, training, skills, and personal information. Its content and appearance are very important. Your resume will create the first impression the interviewer will have of you. You will want to create a resume that an employer will read. Know that there are many styles of resumes, and as your career advances, your resume will become more detailed. Regardless of how much you must report, make your duties your greatest accomplishments.

Important Resume Facts to Know

- Limit your resume to one page, if possible.
- Keep sentences brief.
- Use simple everyday language.
- Do not write in paragraphs. Bullet points are best.
- Be specific.
- Include your achievements.
- Be honest. Do not exaggerate.
- Do not speak of salary or wages, unless asked.
- Use resume stationery in white, ivory, or gray.
- 12-point Times New Roman font.
- Use spell check and proofread when finished.

High School students with little or no work experience should have a resume when applying for work. Although you do not have a lot of experience, it is a good idea for the following reasons:

- It shows the employer you are interested enough in the job to put forth an extra effort.
- It indicates that you know how to conduct yourself in a professional manner.
- It gets the job done.

A winning resume will always grab the attention of the reader:

- It shows why they should hire you by focusing on your accomplishments.
- It is easy to read.
- Each section should be distinct.
- It is neatly typed, without misspelled words or grammatical errors.
- It is printed on resume-quality white, ivory, or gray paper.

PARTS OF A RESUME

Heading

Centering at the top of your stationery, leaving a one-inch margin, type your name on the top line, your address on the second line, city, state, and zip code on the third line, then, your telephone number and e-mail address on the last line.

Objective

It is important that you have an objective. In a short sentence or two tell the kind of job you are looking for. Ex: "Seeking a full-time position in … or if you do not have any experience, then use: Seeking an entry-level position in …"

Education

Identifying your education shows that you are capable of learning. Starting with your most recent school, write the school's name, city, and state, date of completion, and the degree or certificate awarded. Under each school list courses you took that are directly related to the job you are applying for and class rank or GPA. Omit things that you feel would be of no interest to the interviewer.

Skills and Abilities

Limiting each to one line, list skills you have experience in and the area of the prospective position you are applying for.

Work Experience

You will begin with your most recent employer, including on the first line, the last date of employment or if you are still there you will write, "Present", then, you will indicate your title, the name of the employer, and the company's city and state. Directly under that line, explain your job description. (What your responsibilities were)

School Activities

If you did not participate in any extracurricular activities, leave this section out. In this area you would list clubs you are a member of, sports teams, offices held, etc.

References

References should be placed on your application only. Under this title, type "Provided Upon Request". Relatives and friends are not to be used as professional references. Include former employers, teachers, counselors, and anyone else you may have worked with professionally.

Evon A. Carrington
119 West 28th Street
New York, New York 75928
892-725-6348   e-mail address

Objective:

Seeking an entry-level position in the retail industry where I will obtain experience in marketing and business operations.

Skills:

- Outstanding skills in written and oral communications
- Detailed organizational skills
- Willingness to learn and hard working
- Knowledge of business operations

Education:

Summerville High School, Pasadena, NY

Senior, Graduation Date-June 2010

Significant Courses: Economics, Business Management

School Activities

Debate Team

Computer Graphics

Work Experience:

The Classic Dress Shop- 2009 to Present

Sales Associate

Sales associates' duties included maintaining the department inventory of designer wear. Keeping the racks and display tables stocked with current merchandise and current sales advertisement signs.

The Gourmet Burger-2008 to 2009

Cook

Responsibilities included seasoning, cooking, and preparing gourmet burgers for an upscale hamburger restaurant. Duties also included restocking prep counters and keeping inventory records.

Volunteer Community Experiences

Special Events Organizer – Coordinator of birthday and anniversary celebrations. Plan activities and organize events.

Summer Camp Counselor – Youth programs/group leader and maintenance services.

References: Upon request

COVER LETTERS

Cover letters are necessary when sending your resume in the mail. Many companies today require electronic resumes but should also include a cover letter. Your cover letter should be short and precise. Its purpose is to obtain an interview, not tell a lengthy story. The focus should be on your qualifications and setting up an interview.

There are two types of cover letters - Specific and General. The specific cover letter is directed at a specific company, specific person, and identified position. The letter should personally address the company's needs. This type of letter sends a positive message to the prospective employer that you are truly interested and may possibly be a good candidate because you took the time to research the specifics.

A general cover letter is often addressed "To Whom It May Concern" or "Dear Employer." This type of letter focuses more on your qualifications, hoping that a position will be available to utilize your expertise. Using this format may not get you to the top of the career ladder.

The sample cover letter on the next page will help you when preparing your own cover letters. There are five parts to every business letter.

- Heading - Your address and date
- Inside Address - Whom you are sending the letter to
- Salutation - Where the greeting is placed. Ex. Dear Mr., Mrs., Ms. _____
- Body - Placement for your message
- Signature - Your first and last name typed four spaces down, then, sign

SAMPLE COVER LETTER

March 10, 2010

Ms. Janice Shueller
The Blain Company
452 South Avenue
Clare, Illinois 89214

Dear Ms. Shueller:

Sandy Lester, the director of Human Resources, suggested that I contact you about the position of the junior buyer that is open within your company. I am requesting to be considered as an applicant for this position. My resume is enclosed.

I have been working since September of 2009 as an assistant to the head buyer for the Sakz Store in Illinois. I've had the opportunity to develop skills in merchandising and to learn many aspects of marketing. My resume' will provide a complete detailed overview of my experience and the skills I can bring to your company.

Your reputation in the retail industry is proven as one of the top companies and I am especially interested in pursuing a career in the buyer training program. I believe employment with your company would offer me a great opportunity to use my skills and advance in my career as well as be an asset to your company.

I look forward to hearing from you soon. I can be reached at 821-482-9673.

Sincerely,

Evon Carrington

Enclosure

HOW TO COMPLETE A JOB APPLICATION

Now that you have studied the specifics of the process of getting a job, let's review the application process. Although it's a simple process when completing an application, just be reminded that after signing it, it becomes a legal document. Being careful not to make any mistakes, be truthful. Providing false information will call for immediate termination.

Job Application Tips

Here are some tips for completing a job application:

- Prepare all the information you will need the night before and place in your portfolio. (Previous jobs you've had; first and last names of references: addresses, telephone numbers, dates of graduation, etc.)
- Be sure to go alone when filling out your application.
- Use a black pen. Do not borrow one and do not use a pencil.
- Take your social security card. Copies may be required.
- Read the directions carefully. If the direction says print, be sure to do so.
- Be sure to not leave any questions unanswered. If a question does not apply to your situation, write "N/A" or place a short dash in the space.
- Be sure to sign the application.
- Read over everything before turning your application in.
- Be neat. Do not mark through mistakes, use messy erasures or correction fluid.
- Be pleasant and friendly. Maintain eye contact. Smile. Be appreciative.
- Ask what will take place next and how you can get an interview. What is the application review process? Ask about when you can follow up.
- Be sure to call back.
- Remember to smile give a firm handshake and be on your best behavior.

EXERCISE 9.5: PROSPECTIVE EMPLOYER LIST

Looking for a job is a full-time job. When searching for a job, you should keep track of your contacts with each employer. Use the form below to keep up with your contacts. Feel free to make copies of this form to use when setting appointments.

Company Name: _____

Interviewer/Contact Person: _____

Address: _____ Telephone: _____

Kind of Company: _____

Position Available: _____

Date of Interview: _____ Time of Interview: _____

Notes:

INTERVIEW APPEARANCE

There is only one chance to make a first impression. This should be first on your list for making a lasting impression on the interviewer. Looking professional does not require you to physically look a particular way or have a great deal of money. Presentation of neatness will get you noticed along with your knowledge of the job you are applying for. You should dress according to age appropriateness and job type.

- Black, brown, gray, or navy are the look for professional dress.
- Wear a suit (jacket, skirt, and blouse or a blazer over a dress)
- Skirt and dress lengths should end just above the knee.
- Avoid low-cut necklines.
- Choose fabrics that will avoid a wrinkle appearance.
- Always wear a blouse or camisole under your jacket.

Very modest jewelry should be worn to compliment your outfit. Large costume jewelry should never be worn. One set of earrings, limits hand jewelry, bracelets, etc. No scarves.

- Always wear pantyhose. Skin color is most acceptable.
- Wear closed-toe shoes, medium height and clean.
- Avoid loud nail polish and lengthy nails. Manicured.
- Keep to daytime make-up, subtle to the color.
- Limit eyeshadow.
- Hair should be clean and styled conservatively.
- Deodorant is a must.
- Cologne should not be worn.
- Avoid signs of body piercing and tattoos.

Be sure to avoid eating foods that have onions or anything else that has an odor that is hard to get rid of prior to your interview.

INTERVIEWING TECHNIQUES

When preparing for your interview, be sure to prepare at least one week in advance.

- Have a typed resume, neatly printed with no errors in your portfolio.
- Research the company's history so that you have something to talk about when you are asked.
- Know something about the position.
- Go to bed early so that you look rested.
- Dress professionally.
- Make sure your appearance is neat - hair, hands, scent, makeup
- Know your travel route before the day of your interview so that you are punctual.
- Take an extra copy of your resume with you.
- Take a notebook and a black pen with you.
- Visit the restroom before entering your appointment.

During the Interview

- Be sure to arrive earlier enough to not be late. At least 15 to 20 minutes early is good.
- Maintain casual eye contact.
- Sit up straight but be relaxed; not too relaxed.
- Answer questions in a positive manner.
- Indicate your flexibility and eagerness.
- Talk about your qualifications, stability, reliability, and good attendance.
- Stay on track.
- Ask questions in a professional manner when you don't understand.
- Ask questions about the company or position which are not clear.
- Be sure to ask for the job! Employers want to hire someone who wants to work for them.
- Have a pen and paper handy for jotting down notes.
- Know when the interview is over.

After the Interview

- Follow up with a thank-you note; within one week.
- Make the appropriate calls/inquiries discussed in the interview.
- Evaluate all aspects of the interview. What did you do well?

- What do you need to improve?
- Prepare for your next interview.

Some Things Not to Do

- Never let them see you sweat.
- Never discuss personal issues.
- Do not ask too soon about salary and benefits. Allow the interviewer the opportunity to present this subject.
- Do not chew gum or have mints.
- Do not be negative about your previous employer. Always speak positively!
- Never put yourself down.
- Do not get into challenging conversations with the interviewer.
- Do not provide false information.

Exercise 9.6: Frequently Asked Interview Questions

- Tell me about yourself.
- Why do you want this job?
- What are your career goals?
- What are your strengths and weaknesses?
- How would you describe yourself?
- How would your present employer describe you?
- How many times were you tardy or absent from school last year?
- How can you contribute to this company?
- What achievements have given you the most satisfaction? Why?
- Do you work well under pressure?
- Why did you leave your last job?
- Why should this company hire you?
- Do you prefer working alone or with others?
- What kind of boss do you prefer working for?
- What subjects in school did you like best? Least?
- How does family fit into your career goals?

Write how you would answer any of the above questions.

_____

_____

_____

_____

_____

_____

_____

_____

_____

_____

QUESTIONS YOU CAN ASK DURING AN INTERVIEW

- What would be my responsibilities?
- How would my performance be assessed?
- How would I be supervised?
- What are the opportunities for advancement?
- Is there a training program?
- Whom would I be working with?
- Is travel required in this position?
- What would I do during a typical day?
- What sort of dress code do you have?
- What are the work hours?
- Does this position require overtime?
- What is the company's history.
  (The interviewer would like to know that you researched the company)

Remember, you should allow the interviewer to introduce salary and benefits. Don't spend a lot of time asking a lot of questions about this subject because if you are seriously considered the opportunity will present itself.

FOLLOW-UP LETTER
(THANK YOU LETTER)

After your interview, it is professionally appropriate to write a follow-up letter (commonly known as a thank you letter).

Why should you write a thank you letter?

A simple thank-you letter by U.S. mail or e-mail could help you stand out from the competition. A thank-you letter will keep your name fresh in the manager's mind. It will show the interviewer your professionalism and how much you'd like to have the job. It could also get you a second interview.

How long should the thank you letter be?

You should keep the thank-you letter short and to the point. A sample letter is provided on the next page as a guide for you to structure your letter. The sample letter will help you when you write your own letter. Be sure to keep the following things in mind:

1. Use the appropriate letter heading addresses, and date. (Be sure it is free of errors)
2. The letter should be addressed to the interviewer by name. (Contact the company for the correct spelling)
3. The body of the letter should be structured as follows:
   - *First Paragraph*: Thank the interviewer for the interview. Be sure to
   - remind the interviewer when you interviewed and the position you interviewed for.
   - *Second Paragraph*: Add additional information about yourself, your skills, and/or the reasons why you're the one for the job.
   - *Third Paragraph*: As agreed in the interview, mention when you will call and express again your interest in the job.
   - *Closing*: Use the appropriate closing for your letter, like "Sincerely."

How soon should I send the letter?

You should send the thank-you letter within a week of your interview. You will want the letter to reach the interviewer before he or she forgets you.

How important is it to follow up by telephone?

A personal telephone call tells the interviewer how interested you are in the job. It shows your persistence and implies that you will be a worker who will get the job done.

SAMPLE THANK-YOU LETTER

June 28, 2010

Ms. Susan M. White
Cramer Company
8941 Willingham Street
Los Vegas, Nevada 75264

Dear Ms. White:

Thank you for meeting with me, regarding the position of Senior Accountant with the Cramer Company. I was especially excited to learn more about the history of the company. This knowledge has certainly enhanced my interest in working for one of the star companies.

Considering my extensive experience in the full spectrum of accounting, I feel that I can lead the Accounting Department up to standard. Bringing the company into the black margin is my specialty and by hiring me, I would be an asset to your company.

Ms. White, as promised I will contact you by Thursday next week. I would be pleased to provide further information if needed to help your company reach a positive decision regarding my employment.

Thank you again for your consideration.

Sincerely,

Karen Friendly

EXERCISE 9.7: TEST YOUR JOB SEARCH KNOWLEDGE

1. What is a resume?

2. What is the purpose of a resume?

3. List the six main parts of a resume.

   _____   _____

   _____   _____

   _____   _____

4. A _____ _____ should always accompany your resume.

5. It is appropriate to send a _____ _____ _____ after your interview.

6. When should you send a _____ _____ _____?
   Answer: _____

7. Instead of listing your references on your resume, you should type
   _____ _____ _____.

8. Name the two types of cover letters.

   _____ _____

9. What is aptitude?

   _____

10. Name six qualities employers like.

   _____   _____

   _____   _____

   _____   _____

Looking at your checkbook balance can define your worth.

—Gwen Gistarb

Segment X

Keeping Your Eyes on Your Financial Wealth

Objective:

the mother will...
Guide their daughters to selecting financial institutions and services that will best meet their financial needs.

BUDGETING AND SAVING

ONCE YOU BEGIN WORKING, you must begin thinking about your economic life. To plan effectively, you will need enough income to cover your expenses. When doing this you should plan a budget. Keeping a budget will keep your financial life on track. Planning to save and spend money based on your income allows you to separate the amount needed to keep the house running, how much you will save, and what is available to spend on entertainment activities as well as shopping. Creating a budget form is the only way you will be able to reach your financial goals.

When setting up your budget form, there are two types of expenses you will identify.

1. *Fixed Expenses* – expenses that are the same each month
2. *Flexible Expenses* – expenses that vary in amount each month

Read the story on the next page to test your knowledge when completing a budget form.

ALAN AND TRACI'S STORY

A LAN AND TRACI MET during their sophomore year in college and got married last year just after graduating. Neither of them has located jobs in their profession, so they are still working in the same hourly wage jobs they had while in college. They have prepared a budget but are having trouble saving money for their future goals. They would like to take a vacation next year to celebrate their one-year anniversary. Their travel agency has told them about a 4-day cruise to Cancun, New Mexico that includes hotel and airfare for $1200.00 from Atlanta. They would like to take an additional $1000.00 for meals, shopping, and entertainment. When totaling their prospective expenses, they would need $2,200.00 for the trip. Their anniversary is only nine months away.

Using the figures identified on the next page, fill in the monthly budget form. List the first budget amount that was decided upon in the column marked, "Planned." Then, list the actual expenses they incurred during the month, "Actual." You will decide whether each item is a fixed or flexible expense. Place each item in the appropriate space on the budget form. Alan and Traci's net monthly income combined is $4,000.00.

EXERCISE 10.1: BUDGETING

Alan and Traci's Monthly Budgeted Expenditures

Rent	$995.00	Personal Care	$200.00
Electricity	179.00	Gas and Oil	200.00
Car Payment(s)	875.00	Medical Care	100.00
Telephone (Home)	67.00	Entertainment	200.00
Cellular Phone	125.00	Clothing	150.00
Car Insurance	298.00	Gifts and Contributions	100.00
Grocery	450.00		

Alan and Traci's Actual Expenditures for This Month

Rent	$995.00	Personal Care	$120.00
Electricity Bill	250.00	Gas and Oil	123.00
Car Payment	875.00	Medical Care	340.00
Telephone Bill	65.00	Entertainment	100.00
Cellular Bill	235.00	Clothing	100.00
Car Insurance	298.00	Gifts and Contributions	75.00
Grocery	350.00		

Monthly Budget Form

		Monthly Net Income $4,000.00		
Fixed Expenses	Planned	Actual	Under/ Overage	Notes
Flexible Expenses				
Totals				
Savings				

Will Allen and Traci be able to take a vacation? _____

How much will they be able to save? _____

This actual is for one month and each month thereafter may be more or less, so what can they do to assure that they will be able to save enough by the end of the one-year goal?

Understanding Your Paycheck Stub

WHEN YOU RECEIVE YOUR paycheck, you will also receive an attachment that details all the information about your salary deductions. Many companies provide this information electronically for your convenience. Here you will see most of the information you will need to know about your wages. For example, your social security number, employee identification number, date-to-date period worked, your salary rate, overtime, if any, deductions such as taxes, Medicare, insurance, loans, and all the other deductions made. Paycheck stubs may be designed differently depending on the company. With a paycheck stub, everything is clear, eliminating or minimizing the possibility of confusion and complaints.

Employee's Statement of Earnings and Deductions Retain for your records												
Check Stub												
Tot al Hours	Earnings			Total		Deductions					Net Amount	Period Ending
	Regular	Overtime				F.I.CA	Fede ral w/h Tax	State w/h Tax	Medicare			

EXERCISE 10.2: PAYROLL DEDUCTION ACTIVITY

Use the check stub below to answer the following questions.

	**Employee's Statement of Earnings and Deductions Retain for your records**

Check Stub

Total Hours	Earnings				Total		Deductions								Net Amount		Period Ending
	Regular		Overtime				F.I.C.A.		Federal w/h Tax		State w/h Tax		Medicare				
35	300	00				300	00	13	40	21	00	6	99	3	99	159	72	10-10-10

1. What is the gross pay? _____

2. What is the net pay? _____

3. What does F.I.C.A stand for? _____

4. How much is taken out for F.I.C.A. _____

5. How much is deducted for federal taxes? _____

6. How much is deducted for state taxes? _____

7. How much is deducted for social security taxes? _____

What is the total amount deducted? _____

THE USE OF FINANCIAL INSTITUTIONS AND SERVICES

AFTER RECEIVING YOUR PAYCHECK, you will deposit it into a bank account. What is a bank account? "A bank account is a financial account with a financial institution that records the financial transactions between the customer and the bank." You should shop around before deciding which financial institution will provide you with the best choice of banking services. There are several types of financial institutions offering a broad range of services, such as Commercial Banks, Savings and Loan Associations, Credit Unions, and Mutual Savings Banks.

Shopping for a Bank

When making your choice of where to open an account you will be most interested in a personal checking account. It provides a safe place to keep cash and convenient way to buy goods and services and to pay bills. Mostly this type of account provides a record of spending and receipt of payments, which will provide a way of tracking all your financial transactions.

Upon shopping for a checking account, the following questions may be helpful when making the best choice:

- What is the minimum deposit required?
- What is the minimum balance required for a regular account?
- What is the penalty for failing to maintain the minimum balance?
- Is there a maintenance fee?
- What fees are charged for different services and accounts?
- What are the fees for a returned check?
- Do you offer overdraft protection for accounts?

Opening a Checking Account

Upon receiving your first check, opening a checking account requires only a few simple steps. At most banks certain policies may apply if you are under 18 years of age. Some banks may require you to have a parent or guardian on the account with you and others may not.

While opening an account, you will be asked to sign a signature card. Be sure that your signature is how you plan to sign all your checks because this is the only one the bank will honor on your checks and deposit slips. You may want someone else to have check cashing privileges on your account, if so that person will need to sign a signature card. Understand that when you share an account with someone, it becomes a joint account. This requires a clear understanding of who will write checks and how your records of transactions will be kept.

When you open a checking account, you will receive a small book of checks that will get you started. These checks will be blank except for your new account number. You will use these checks while waiting for your personalized checks to arrive. You will order your personalized checks at the same time of opening your account. Your new checks will be printed with your name, address, and account number and include a register for keeping track of your transactions.

Because laws change so often, speak with your personal banker about the personal credit, debit, and automatic teller machine cards when you open your account.

MAKING A DEPOSIT

WHEN DEPOSITING A CHECK into your account, fill out a deposit slip as a record of the transaction. Your deposit slip identifies what is being deposited; currency, coins, or checks and the amount of each item, totaling at the bottom. Follow these steps when filling out a deposit slip.

- Write the correct date.
- Enter the amount of money being deposited. Currency - the amount of cash in dollars; Coins – the number of coins to be deposited; Checks – checks may begin on the front side of the deposit slip, but there are more spaces on the back of the deposit slip. (Total the amount on the back to transfer to the front of the slip)
- Total the amount of currency, coins, and checks to be deposited.
- You will write the total on the line opposite Sub-total.
- You may want to withdraw cash at the same time you make a deposit, enter this amount opposite Less Cash. This will require a signature on the line under the date if you want cash back from your deposit.
- Now enter the actual amount you are depositing opposite the Total deposit.
- To keep an accurate balance, you should immediately record the amount deposited in your checkbook registers.

Sample Deposit Slip

SAMPLE

Jerry Smith

1987 Avenue H

Anywhere, USA 88216

Date _____ 20_____

_____

Sign here only if cash received from deposit

Miahdlan National Bank

Anywhere, USA 5920

Currency			
Coins			
Checks			
Total from other side			
Sub Total			
Less Cash			
Total Deposit			

XXXXXXXXXX   XXXXXXXXXX

ENDORSING CHECKS

BEFORE YOU CAN CASH or deposit your check you must endorse it. Endorsing a check is the same as signing your name on the back left end just as the check is written out to you. The endorsement allows you to cash or deposit it into your account. There are three ways you can accomplish the endorsement.

- Specialty Endorsement - Pay to the order of, then, sign your name underneath
- Restrictive Endorsement - For Deposit Only -then, sign your name underneath
- Blank Endorsement - Sign your name

Endorse Here

_____

Do Not Write, Stamp, or Sign Below This Line

WRITING CHECKS

UNDERSTANDING THE IMPORTANCE OF the pre-printed information on your check will guide you to writing checks accurately and completely. Below is a diagram of all of the information you will find on a check. Review the diagram, then, read the section below to learn the parts of a check.

Identification of the Parts of a Check

1. Check number.
2. The "Pay to the Order Of" – This line is where you write the name of the person or company to whom you will give the check.
3. The date.
4. Your name and address.

5. Name and address of Codes – The state where the bank is located and the Federal Reserve Bank that will handle this check.

6. The signature line – Remember to sign your check the same as you did on the signature card.

7. Routing Number

8. The memo section – Optional. You can make a note to yourself the reason for writing the check.

9. The dollar amount in words - Begin writing the amount of the check in words as far to the left as possible, writing the cents amount as a fraction (23/100), then draw a line to the end of the space.

10. Numerical amount of check.

11. Account number

It is important that you write your checks in ink for your own protection. Pencil is unprofessional and could easily be erased, which means someone could alter your check.

BALANCING YOUR CHECKBOOK

WHEN YOU RECEIVE YOUR bank statement in the mail, you will compare all the checks you've written during the month. You can also retrieve your account information via the internet. A bank statement is a record of checks, ATM transactions, deposits, and charges on your account.

Each month when receiving your bank statement, it is important to make sure your record agrees with the bank. This is called reconciling your bank statement. It will usually include a summary of the activity in your account and the following items:

- Opening Balance – the amount in your account at the beginning of the bank statement period.
- Deposits Received – the date and amount of each deposit during the statement period.
- Checks paid – the date and amount of each check paid out of your account during the statement period.
- ATM/Debit transactions – the date and amount of any withdrawals or deposits made at the ATM during the statement period.
- Other charges – the date and amount charged for checks, overdrafts, and service fees.
- Closing balance – the amount of money in your account at the end of the statement period.

Below the summary is a detailed record of each check, deposit, and ATM transaction, as well as a running balance of your account.

Sample Bank Statement

Look at the sample bank statement on the next page.

```
HCBank                          Statement of Account
Web-site address           Last Statement: February 30, 2022
                            This Statement: March 30, 2022
                         Total days in statement Period: 31

Sandra C. Schmidth
45871 Karen Street
My Statement, Account 99758
```

Account Number: 1203654089

Beginning Balance	Deposits and Credit		Checks/Withdrawals and /Debits		Ending Balance
	No.	Total Amount	No.	Total Amount	
$420.73	2	$295.00	6	$304.62	$527.42

Checking Account Transactions

Date	Debits	Credits	Description
03/05		$225.00	Deposit
03/25		$70.00	Deposit

Checks

Date	Check No.	Amount	Date	Check No.	Amount
03/02	521	$25.10	03/15	524	$15.00
03/05	522	$10.52	03/20	525	$25.79
03/11	523	$32.29	03/27	526	$68.41

Reconciling Your Bank Statement

Bank statements are designed differently, depending on the bank. However, the information on the bank statement and balancing worksheet below, of course, will be the same when guiding you through the process of reconciliation. When reconciling your bank statement, the first step is to complete the following activities:

- Compare the canceled checks listed on the statement with the checks in hand.
- Compare the canceled checks with those recorded in your checkbook register.
- Compare the deposits in your register with those on the statement.

Sample Balancing Worksheet

How to Reconcile Your Account

Balance shown on
Bank Statement .... $ _____

Add Deposits
Not on Statement + $ _____

_____

_____

Sub-Total .... $ _____

Subtract Checks
Issued But

Check No.	Not on Statement
_____	$ _____
_____	_____
_____	_____
_____	_____
_____	_____
_____	_____
_____	_____
_____	_____
_____	_____

Total .... -$ _____

Balance .... -$ _____

*The above balance should be the same as the up-to-date balance in your checkbook.

EXERCISE 10.3: DEPOSIT TICKET & CHECK

Managing a checking account involves several procedures. Let's begin with you having an account at North Mansion Bank. You just received your paycheck and need to make a deposit and write a check to a dress shop. After doing so enter your transactions in your checkbook register.

Make out a deposit slip for your paycheck in the amount of $102.51 and $25.00 currency you received for babysitting. The date is March 28, 2010.

	81-1892		
Lindsey Cappers	Currency		
2385 Avenue G	Coins		
Anywhere, USA 78511			
Date	Checks		
_____ 20 _____			
_____			
Sign here only if cash received from deposit			
	Total from other side		
$ North Mansion Bank	Sub Total		
Anywhere, USA 48961	Less Cash		
	Total Deposit		
XXXXXXXXX XXXXXXXXXX			

Write a check for $50.00 to pay for your dress from the Dress Hut.
The date is March 30, 2010.

		527
Lindsey Cappers		
2385 Avenue G		
Anywhere, USA 78511	Date _____	
Pay to the		
order of _____ $_____		
_____ Dollars		
North Mansion Bank		
Anywhere, USA 48961		
For _____ _____		
XXXXXXXXX XXXXXXXXXX 0527		

EXERCISE 10.4: CHECKBOOK REGISTER

Record your deposit and check for your new dress. Remember to balance your checkbook.

Record all charges or credits that affect your account								
Number	Date	Description of Transaction	Payment/ Debit		Fee	Deposit/Credit		Balance
								$ 420	73
521	3/2	Telephone	25	10					
522	3/5	Drug Store	10	52					
	3/10	Deposit				225	00		
523	3/11	Sporting Store	32	29					
524	3/15	Dan Hefty	15	00					
525	3/20	Computer Palace	25	79					
	3/25	Deposit				70	00		
526	3/27	The Men Store	68	41					

EXERCISE 10.5: BANK STATEMENT/BALANCING WORKSHEET

Your bank statement arrived today, April 10, 2010, so you now need to reconcile your account.

Checking Account Transactions

Date	Debits	Credits	Description Deposit Deposit
03/05		$225.00	
03/25		$70.00	

Checks

Date	Check No.	Amount	Date	Check No.	Amount
03/02	521	$25.10	03/15	524	$15.00
03/05	522	$10.52	03/20	525	$25.79
03/11	523	$32.29	03/27	526	$68.41

The deposit you made and the check you wrote earlier in this activity are not shown in the bank statement. However, you did record them in your check register. Check the accuracy of your recordkeeping against the bank statement by filling in the worksheet below. The balance on the worksheet should be the same as the balance on your check register.

Balancing Worksheet

Balance shown on

    Bank Statement.. $_____

Add Deposits
    Not on Statement   +$_____

    _____

    _____

    Sub-Total.. $_____

	Check No.	**Subtract Checks Not on Statement**
	_____	$_____
	_____	_____
	_____	_____
	_____	_____
	_____	_____
		_____

    Total...................................... -$_____

    Balance.................................... *$_____

*The above balance should be the same as the up-to-date balance in your checkbook.

From the Author
It's Time to Let Go

I'T'S BEEN MANY YEARS since I've had to let go, allowing my daughter to find her own way. She's all grown up now and I am proud to say she's made me very proud. Now, I can witness her raising her two daughters with many of the same techniques I used on her. I continue to stand in the shadows of motherhood to witness my teachings put into play. Our relationship is just what a mother and daughter should share through the disagreements of the teenage years and blossoming into a friendship that will last a lifetime.

Molding every step of my mirrored image, and happily "saying, wow what a wonderful person I've made." I helped her take her first steps while she learned to run on her own, I watched her learn to ride her first bicycle when she learned to race on her own, I taught her to drive her first car and now she can guide her life into whichever direction she chooses to go. It wasn't easy letting go, but how proud I am to see my daughter who has grown to be the perfect lady my mother raised me to be. How sweet the song is in my heart. As years have passed, I welcome the honor of being called, Grand Mommy. Her little ladies will walk in her footsteps as she watches them grow to find their own way and mommy feels the same heartache I felt when I had to let go.

I am a firm believer that children are the most precious gift a parent will receive in a lifetime, whether it is a daughter or a son. I had the pleasure of experiencing both. Of course, daughters are difficult, but what joy I've had dressing my live little baby doll. Teaching her to dress and waiting to see what she would choose, then correcting her plaids and stripes until she learned her fabrics and colors. Remembering what my mother warned me of when raising children is that they will inherit not only your good qualities but will also demonstrate the ones we'd like to keep a secret. Let me just say my firry, talking back little me reappeared.

Families are not complete until children are added. Enjoy the frustrations, respect their individuality, listening to their concerns and conflicts that you will experience as forever-lasting memories are made. Now, you can let go if you can relate to the many stories, metaphors, and information provided to you in my book. Remembering that you will never be free from your daughter's needs so just consider yourself on call for a lifetime.

A Mother reminds her child...

"God bless the child
who has her own."

— Referenced from Billie Holiday, Arthur Herzog, Jr. (1939)

ANSWER GUIDE

Upon making the decision to become a parent, there are many responsibilities one will encounter. In the beginning, you will be responsible for providing constant care for 24 hours a day, seven days per week, and three hundred sixty-five days a year. You will now be referred to as a **caregiver**. As your child begins to develop her own personality and learns from all aspects of life, you are responsible for providing structure and guidance while allowing freedom within that structure. This makes you the **guidance provider** in the home. When taking on such an important task, mothers creatively demonstrate many roles in their daughters' first years. Parents are the first **teacher** their child will know, providing an enthusiastic attitude toward learning activities. Preparing your child with the best possible educational environment that matches their needs will support your efforts as an **educational provider**. As a **social director**, you will also provide social activities for your child, which will help them to gain knowledge of social skills such as sharing and good manners. Also, by acting as a **communicator**, your child will know that they are loved through both words and touch. Speaking to them in a pleasant voice, rather than a bossy demanding tone will allow you to listen to their every concern. Being an **empathizer** is to understand and being considerate of children's feelings. Understanding outbursts of anger and crying can help them deal with everyday issues better regardless of their magnitude. Many parents aren't aware that they are their child's main **resource person**. You must answer the many questions they may have, being patient and understanding. You are also responsible for maintaining proper schedules of rest and exercise for your child as well as vaccinations and always being aware of the symptoms of illness, can perform first aid and be prepared to obtain medical services if needed. Basically, you are their **healthcare provider**. Providing nutritious foods at properly scheduled feeding times and being aware of their nutritional needs as they develop will require your expertise as a **nutrition provider**. You are the **assistant decision-maker** in their lives. You are to help your child in making decisions, teaching them the decision-making process. Only to assist, allowing them to arrive at their own decision. You are their **clothing provider**, providing them with clothing that is comfortable, allows movement, and provides protection from the elements. You also teach them cleanliness and how to maintain a clean environment. For many years your title among others, will also be their **chauffeur**, transporting your daughter to the doctor, school, parties, and many other activities as they grow. Demonstrate positive self-esteem by helping your child to feel good about who she is. Providing support and love at all times, whether she achieves or fails. Support her desire to try again. This will surely demonstrate that you are her **supporter**. Parents should **safeguard** their children to provide a safe environment for growth and development.

1. Condom
2. Epididymis.
3. IUD
4. Withdrawal
5. Infertility
6. Miscarriage
7. Menstruation
8. Ovaries
9. Gene
10. Endometrium.
11. Urethra.
12. Vas Deferens.
13. Tubal Ligation
14. Fallopian Tube.
15. Abortion
16. Chromosomes.
17. Sperm; egg
18. Egg
19. Testes
20. Ovulation.

EXERCISE 5.3 TAKING RESPONSIBILITY WORD SEARCH HIDDEN WORD, PAGE 72 RESPONSIBILITY

1. A brief concise document that presents and effectively sells your credentials.

2. The purpose of a resume is to get an interview, admission to graduate school, consideration for a scholarship or other professional purposes.

3. Name, address, contact information
    Education
    Job Objective
    Honors and Activities
    Work Experience
    Special Skills and Abilities

4. cover letter

5. thank you letter

6. thank you letter? Answer: within one week.

7. Upon Request

8. Specific Cover Letter; General Cover Letter

9. Your natural ability to do something or your quickness to learn.

10. Enthusiasm
    Initiative
    Team Player
    Abide by Company Dress Code
    Follow Policies and Procedures
    Dependability

Monthly Net Income $4,000.00

Fixed Expenses	Planned	Actual
Rent	995.00	995.00
Cars	875.00	875.00
Insurance	298.00	298.00
Flexible Expenses		
Electric Bill	179.00	250.00
Telephone Bill	67.00	65.00
Cellular Bill	125.00	235.00
Grocery Bill	450.00	350.00
Personal Care	200.00	120.00
Gas and Oil	200.00	123.00
Medical Care	100.00	340.00
Entertainment	200.00	100.00
Clothing	150.00	100.00
Gifts, etc.	100.00	75.00
Totals	$3939.00	$3926.00
Savings	$61.00	$74.00

1. $300.00
2. $159.72
3. Federal Insurance Contribution Act
4. $13.40
5. $21.00
6. $6.99
7. $3.99
8. $45.38

81-1892

Lindsey Cappers
2385 Avenue G
Anywhere, USA 78511

Date March 28, 2022

Currency		25	00
Coins			
		102	51
Checks			
	Total from other side		
Sub Total		$ 127	51
Less Cash			
Total Deposit		$ 127	51

Sign here only if cash received from deposit

$ North Mansion Bank
Anywhere, USA 48961

xxxxxxxxx   xxxxxxxxxx

Lindsey Cappers   527
2385 Avenue G
Anywhere, USA 78511   Date March 30, 2022

Pay to the
order of Dress Hut $ 38.80

Thirty-eigth & 80/100 --Dollars

North Mansion Bank
Anywhere, USA 48961

For _____   _____

XXXXXXXXX   XXXXXXXXXX   0527

EXERCISE 10.4: CHECKBOOK REGISTER, PAGE 151

Number	Date	Description of Transaction	Payment/ Debit		Fee	Deposit/Credit $ 420 73		Balance	
521	3/2	Telephone	25	10				395	63
522	3/5	Drug Store	10	52				385	11
	3/10	Deposit				225	00	610	11
523	3/11	Sporting Store	32	29				577	82
524	3/15	Dan Hefty	15	00				562	82
525	3/20	Computer Palace	25	79				537	03
	3/25	Deposit				70	00	607	03
526	3/27	The Men Store	68	41				538	62
	3/28	Deposit				127	51	666	13
527	3/30	Dress Hut	50	00				616	13

Record all charges or credits that affect your account

EXERCISE 10.5: BANK STATEMENT/BALANCING WORKSHEET, PAGE 152

Balance shown on
Bank Statement .... $ 527.42

Add Deposits
Not on Statement   + 127.51

Sub-Total .... $ 654.93

	Check No.	Subtract Checks Not on Statement
	527	$38.80

Total.. - $ 38.80
Balance.. $ 616.13

PERMISSIONS

"Reflections" printed by permission of Ella Jefferson.

"A Second Chance" printed by permission of Jamie.

"My Scratch-off Miracle" printed by permission of Shana.

"Perpetrators" printed by permission of Airrass Aog Aod.

"An Effort to Understand" printed by permission of Kathy.

"Facing the World on My Own" printed by permission of Sandi Canady.

"Growing Up Is Hard to Do" printed by permission of Allison.

"Obstacles" printed by permission of Karl.

"Amari's Fish, Jack" printed by permission of Daphne Wills.

"I Should Have Waited" printed by permission of Julie G.

"Disappointed" printed by permission of S. Williams.

"How They Have Changed" printed by permission of Ella Jefferson.

"A Second Call to Duty" printed by permission of Susan A.

"When Children Listen" printed by permission of Gwen Gistarb.

"Forced to Grow Up a Teenage Father" printed by permission of Todd D.

"A Gift from God" printed by permission of Mariah.

"Apology to My Children" printed by A Mother's Love.

Davis, A.S., 2009, Metaphor, pg. 49

Brenda, 2009, Metaphor, pg. 51

L. Jacqui, 2009, Metaphor, pg. 59

To correspond with Gwen Gistarb
you may e-mail her:
gygistarb@gwengistarb.net
or log in to her website at:
www.gwengistarb.net

To order direct:
http://www.litprime.com
http://www.barnesandnoble.com
http://www.amazon.com

For information on booking Gwen for a
speaking engagement:
gygistarb@gwengistarb.net